A WORLD ELSEWHERE

THE NEW AMERICAN FOREIGN POLICY

JAMES CHACE

CHARLES SCRIBNER'S SONS
NEW YORK

FOR SUE AND FOR DAVID

CONTENTS

I do love
My country's good with a respect more tender,
More holy, and profound, than mine own life. . . .
[But] there is a world elsewhere.

CORIOLANUS

I

THE ROOTS OF THE
NEW FOREIGN
POLICY

The balance (of power) was determined by the sword which was thrown in on one side or the other; a balance which was determined by the unstable equilibrium of competitive interests; a balance which was maintained by jealous watchfulness and an antagonism of interest.

—Woodrow Wilson

It is thus a mistake to regard the balance of power as some iniquitous plotting of forces; it was rather an achievement of such a distribution of strength as would render aggression by any single country a policy of the greatest uncertainty and danger.

—Sir Harold Nicolson

ONE

"What have we to do with destiny now?" Bonaparte remarked to Goethe. "Politics are destiny." In foreign policy it should never be forgotten that politics dictate policy—the means however pragmatic and the ends however moral. To try to exclude foreign policy from the realm of politics is to court disaster. To indulge in abstract theories is to become what Palmerston warned against—the Quixote of the world. The politics of a nation, and hence the controlling force of its foreign policy, can of course change direction more rapidly than a policy that has been launched in response to a different political environment. An obsolete foreign policy cannot be lightly discarded; commitments once made are not easily broken. But as the politics of an earlier time may determine the continuation of an outdated foreign policy, so, too, a radically different political atmosphere can make possible changes in foreign policy which then become a legacy for future statesmen.

As the avowedly conservative Richard Nixon directed the foreign policy of the United States in the years following 1968, America moved into an uncharted area of the post-postwar world. It was a world that had already grown obsolete. There are key dates, signalling if not marking the end of the postwar world, just as Einstein's theory of relativity and the beginning of the great European civil war in 1914 foreshadowed the end of the modern world such as we had known it since the Renaissance. The persistence of the na-

5

tion-state in the formulation of foreign policy and the emergence of transnational forces that now chiefly shape our
world have brought into focus the need for a new approach
to foreign affairs. But we can discern the coast ahead only if
we first understand what a long distance we have traveled
over the past quarter century.

In tracing the evolution and termination of the cold war,
1956 was certainly a watershed year since it then became
clear that the United States would respect Eastern Europe
as a Soviet sphere of influence and there would be no more
meaningless talk of "liberation" and "roll-back." It was also
a year that saw Washington and Moscow lined up against
America's wartime European allies, England and France,
over the Suez intervention. From that point on, it was clear
that America's and Europe's perceptions of their respective
vital interests would not necessarily coincide. Though Paris
and London drew opposite conclusions from the American
response to the Suez fiasco—Britain anxious to repair an already anachronistic concept of a "special relationship" with
Washington; France determined to press on with the construction of an independent nuclear force—the basic European response to the events of 1956 was both to recognize
the possibility of a sometime Russo–American partnership
and to forestall any such eventuality by pushing forward toward some form of confederation which would allow the
Europeans freedom of action from the pressures of the superpowers. The Treaty of Rome establishing the Common
Market, the embryo of the European Community, was
signed in 1957 and went into effect in 1958.

Despite the significance of those two traumatic events—
Suez and Hungary—the implications for the future were
not readily apparent as the Eisenhower years drew to a

close. With Richard Nixon as Vice President, the ruthless anticommunism he incarnated still infused the rhetoric of policymakers. Even the abortive attempt by Eisenhower to establish better relations with the then Soviet party chief Nikita Khrushchev—that brief moment in September 1959 when the "spirit of Camp David" hung in the air in the wake of Khrushchev's visit to America—all these signs of thaw quickly disappeared when the 1960 summit meeting in Paris was destroyed by the downing of the American U-2 reconnaissance plane over the Soviet Union and by the recrimination and bitterness that followed.

Yet the bipolar postwar world was breaking apart even as the rhetoric of anticommunism ushered in the high point of the American imperium. The Sino–Soviet split of the early 1960s hardly affected the growing American involvement in Indochina, an involvement justified primarily on the grounds of containing Chinese expansion. The Kennedy administration began ominously with its failure to enforce American hegemony in Cuba at the Bay of Pigs within what had been considered since 1823 as our traditional sphere of influence. Yet such adventurism as Kennedy's was more than matched by the adventurism of Nikita Khrushchev—the cold war, if anything, reached new peaks of violence and danger both in the Berlin crisis of 1961 and, more dramatically, in the October 1962 Cuban missile crisis, when the United States and the Soviet Union brought the world to the edge of nuclear war while the lesser powers were once again reminded of their weakness and their vulnerability.

The year 1963 was a second major turning point, though neither clearly perceived nor enunciated by many of those who directed the foreign policy of the United States. Seemingly omnipotent, the United States during the Cuban missile crisis demonstrated before all the world the threat of its power. As a consequence, the Test-ban Treaty with the Soviet Union marked a recognition of a standoff between the two superpowers.

Furthermore, during the summer of 1963, the breakdown of the talks between Moscow and Peking demonstrated that their strained alliance had finally been stretched to the breaking point. The European diplomatic commentator Richard Lowenthal has since pointed out: with Peking bent on an independent course, "the road to less 'ideological' power politics seemed open everywhere." [1] An era of détente between the United States and Russia was clearly opening up; surely a parallel situation would follow in regard to China. At the same time it seemed reasonable to predict a more independent Japan, and in the event of General de Gaulle's change of heart or departure, an increasingly integrated Europe. Yet these developments did not take place, largely because of what Lowenthal terms "an odd detour of history." This tragic detour was, of course, the Vietnam War. For Washington the cold war had to be fought out on a new battlefield—and the enemy was China.

Had not Mao's heir apparent Lin Piao in 1965 proclaimed a new doctrine of "wars of liberation"? Was not the world a global battlefield where the cities of the plain were to be surrounded and finally conquered by the guerrilla in a kind of twentieth-century game of "Go"?

Soon to be buttressed by his military doctrine of flexible response, President John F. Kennedy warned in his inaugural address, that "we shall pay any price, bear any burden, meet any hardship, support any friend, oppose any foe to assure the survival and success of liberty."

"We will stand as watchmen on the walls of world freedom." These were the words of John F. Kennedy in a speech scheduled to be delivered in Dallas, Texas, on November 22, 1963. At his death the United States found itself in some form of alliance with forty-two countries throughout the globe.

This was the heritage of Lyndon Johnson. Five years later, in a year marked by riots, assassinations, and the commitment of over half a million men to an Asian land war that even General MacArthur had warned against, the cold war had achieved its own apogee. The greatest of the superpowers was caught in an endgame with no major allies. Unsure even of its true adversaries—was it Peking, Moscow, Hanoi, all three?—America's only victory in Indochina could be of the sort which Tacitus described: "Where they could make a desert, they call it peace."

Upon the ruins of Indochina, the United States began its long retreat and prepared for the contraction of its so brief imperium. Finally, even for those who had not already perceived the drift of history, 1968 knelled an end to the cold war. And, ironically, America chose as the liquidator that most redoubtable cold warrior of them all, Richard Nixon. A new American foreign policy was in the making. The politics of the 1970s could not be those of the 1950s and 1960s. And by 1972, there was to be a new legacy that any future president would have to deal with. The traditional policies of the cold war were turned upside down. And once the direction of foreign policy shifts perceptively, it is not only difficult to change course swiftly again; it is also impossible to return to the past.

How, then, has the United States so significantly changed its foreign policy that, despite certain deadly rhetorical hangovers, one can be fairly sure that things will not be as they once were? In 1822, after George Canning, one of Britain's great foreign secretaries, destroyed the Congress system of international government set up by his predecessor Castlereagh at the Congress of Vienna in 1815, he declared with great satisfaction that things were as they should be— "Every nation for itself and God for us all." When Richard Nixon, in his State of the World message in 1972, proclaimed that "our alliances are no longer addressed primarily to the containment of the Soviet Union and China behind an American shield," then the United States truly embarked upon policies that could lead to the creation of a world radically different from what we have known since 1947.

The specifics of most of these changes are already clear: the re-establishment of relations with Communist China, a New Economic Policy which has virtually declared that the dollar can no longer be used as the currency for financing world trade, the conclusion of agreements with the Soviet Union to limit the deployment of weapons of mass destruction, and, above all, the attempt to play the game of balancing the powers on a world scale, the retreat from maintaining a global gendarmerie while pretending that we can maintain our commitments. Though, as I have said, politics have played no small role in forcing these changes, or, at least, in making them possible, the fact is that postwar American foreign policy has been set on a new azimuth. What are the roots of this new foreign policy? To understand not only what has happened but what lies behind it are vital precisely because there is no turning back. The new American foreign policy can develop in either wise or foolish ways. But before we can try to determine the best course for the future, we must first understand what has already been plotted on the chart, a course that even a new navigator must take cognizance of in order to correct it for the better.

TWO

Consistency in politics is neither particularly desirable nor generally possible. Since foreign policy is ultimately dictated by political considerations, changes in foreign policy, though lagging behind political machinations, are often engineered by men whose public statements at one time can sharply conflict with their later public positions. As Talleyrand, the master survivor, put it: "One must always move, and move prudently, with one's age." The stained past, often his own, is the statesman's heritage. John F. Kennedy was the only Democratic Senator who did not vote to censure Senator Joseph McCarthy in 1954, and later ran for the presidency as a man who incarnated the liberal tradition of his party. Nor should it be forgotten that the then Senator Lyndon Johnson, also in 1954, refused to support any plan to send American troops to Indochina. In both Kennedy's and Johnson's cases their changes of heart evolved out of premises to which they felt both their party and their country were committed.

Yet the foreign policy both administrations pursued was a broad continuum of the Truman-Eisenhower years. While the origins of the cold war are certainly rooted in the years of the Truman administration, and the Eisenhower years are often scanted over, it was the legacy of those years which most directly affected the policies of the Kennedy-Johnson administrations. The doctrine of containment of the Soviet Union, enunciated publicly in 1947 by George Kennan in his "Mr. X" article in *Foreign Affairs,* was extended during the Eisenhower administration to a degree which Kennan neither imagined nor intended. What was essential in Kennan's argument was his assertion that "containment of expansive tendencies" be matched by the "adroit and vigilant application of counter-force at a series of constantly shifting geographical and political points." The article was originally part of a paper prepared for Secretary of Defense James Forrestal, and presented in February of that same year. A month later, in March 1947, the Truman Doctrine was promulgated promising military aid to Greece and Turkey. But the Doctrine also contained the ambiguous phrase that the United States should "support free peoples who are resisting attempted subjugation by armed minorities or by outside pressures."

In his *Memoirs,*[2] published twenty years after, Mr. Kennan strongly criticized the Truman Doctrine's interpretation—"terms more grandiose than anything that I, at least, have ever entertained." He regretted that his article should have been misunderstood or used as a basis for the attempted global containment of communism. Mr. Kennan in his *Memoirs* also underlined his own "failure to . . . make clear that the 'containment' of which I was speaking was not something that I thought we could, necessarily, do everywhere successfully, in order to serve the purpose I had in mind."

Actually [he explains] as noted in connection with the Truman Doctrine . . . I distinguished clearly in my own mind between areas that I thought vital to our security and ones that did not seem to fall into this category. My objection to the Truman Doctrine message revolved largely around its failure to draw this distinction.

Finally, and most importantly, Kennan regretted that he did not point out clearly in the "X" article that he had meant "not the containment by military means of a military threat, but the political containment of a political threat." And he emphatically disclaimed any responsibility for being the author of "precisely those features of the Truman Doctrine which I had most vigorously opposed."

Despite the ambiguity of language of the Truman Doctrine, a far broader application of the Kennan policy of "containment" occurred ten years later with the Eisenhower Doctrine. Although the new Doctrine was ostensibly developed in order to cope with the situation in the Middle East after the disastrous 1956 Franco–British Suez expedition, it revealed what British political analyst Anthony Hartley has called "a significant mutation in American policy." [3]

This mutation was an enlargement of an American commitment not only to contain Communist power but to maintain the status quo in any nation even indirectly threatened by communism. The Eisenhower Doctrine stated that not only economic aid would be granted Middle Eastern countries but also American forces "to secure and protect the territorial integrity and political independence of such nations requesting such aid against overt aggression from any nation controlled by international communism."

What resulted, however, was an intervention in Lebanon in 1958, not because this small Levantine country was directly threatened by communism but rather out of a belief that the stability of the country—indeed of the region—was of paramount importance if it could be threatened even indirectly by communism. America's global commitment broadened considerably. Again, as Anthony Hartley has pointed out: "The United States had passed from the military and economic support of countries thought to be more or less directly threatened by Russian or Chinese military power or domestic communist subversion to the more ambitious task of dealing in advance with international trouble anywhere lest it might give an opening for Russian penetration in countries with little political staying-power." [4]

The concept of stability—particularly regional stability —was the great legacy bequeathed by Eisenhower to his successor. Moreover, while the overall policies formulated in the early years of the cold war were expanded by President Truman, Eisenhower's style was significantly different, with significantly different results.

Soon after John Foster Dulles was made Secretary of State in 1952, he was calling for an "agonizing reappraisal"; what this meant was not a re-examination of the assumptions of United States foreign policy but rather a rethinking of our military strategy, particularly in the light of France's hesitation to embrace the concept of a European Defense Community. "Massive retaliation"—the "bigger bang for the buck"—a strategy well-suited to a conservative, budget-minded administration, was to become the fundament of American strategic policy during the decade of the 1950s.

To understand more clearly what actually resulted during the Eisenhower-Dulles era, one must approach the concept of language as a form of action. Not only was there the hyperbolic use of language by Dulles, who spoke of "brink-manship" and "agonizing reappraisals," but the global net-work of alliances and pacts—which proliferated under Dulles—was also a form of rhetoric in action. In fact, pacts, such as the Southeast Asia Treaty Organization (SEATO), the Korean and Taiwan pacts, the somewhat tenuous American support of the Central Treaty Organization in the Middle East (CENTO), were designed to deter—with-out United States military power—Russian and Chinese power in the aftermath of the Korean War. Eisenhower and Dulles were, of course, well aware that the United States was committed by no treaty to go to war without the con-sent of the Congress. For example, consultation among sig-natories was all that the SEATO pact called for. Language became action. Rhetoric became a perverse form of reality.

In fact, the Eisenhower administration was characterized by an avoidance of intervention. With the exception of the rather opera buffa landing on the beaches of Beirut in 1958, Eisenhower refused to intervene: both in Indochina in 1954 after the French defeat at Dien Bien Phu and in 1956 when the Hungarian Revolt seemed to demand American assist-ance. It is important to keep in mind the distinction be-tween rhetoric and reality. During the Eisenhower years, no matter how exalted the level of evangelical preachments, the United States *avoided* military confrontations.

It may well have been the case that the deliberately le-galistic mind of Dulles, as manifested in his treaty arrange-ments, allowed more maneuverability than Presidents Ken-nedy and Johnson availed themselves of. Thus, the rhetoric of the Eisenhower administration was particularly inflated, oftentimes to obscure the actual fact of inaction. Such tutelage was not lost upon Vice President Richard Nixon, who was then being initiated into the higher councils of foreign policymaking.

There were certainly many occasions (one shudders to use the word "opportunities") when American military involvement was a distinct possibility: Korea, the Taiwan Straits, Indochina, Germany, Hungary, Suez, Cuba, and, of course, Lebanon. But, what Richard Rovere has termed Eisenhower's "prudent management"[5] prevented such crises from escalating into war. For example, the danger that the United States would be drawn into a conflict with mainland China by Chiang Kai-shek was a risk Eisenhower was determined to avoid. His recourse was to pledge military aid to Chiang *if* the United States believed that a serious military effort was being made by Peking to invade Taiwan. What was, however, particularly relevant in his methods of avoiding confrontation was his resort to "nuclear blackmail"—a threat used to effect a truce in Korea on terms that Truman could never have accepted.

Eisenhower's decision not to intervene in Indochina was influenced not only by his unwillingness to commit American troops to a land war in Asia but also because the nuclear threat was inappropriate to the enemy. However, in evaluating Eisenhower's performance in foreign affairs, one must remind oneself not only of his belief in his own military judgment. Eisenhower also firmly held the notion that American intervention should be supported by major allies. British Prime Minister Anthony Eden's advice against going into Indochina to assist the French during the debacle of Dien Bien Phu was probably as significant as the military consideration.

Despite his caution when confronted with a demonstrable

crisis, it was under Eisenhower that the American imperium expanded dramatically, and the commitments he made in allowing Dulles to indulge his penchant for pactomania were later to be picked up—with dire consequences.

With the battlefield no longer confined to Europe, with the United States and the Soviet Union recognizing the validity of "the delicate balance of terror," with the United States bound by a network of pacts and "executive agreements," the Kennedy administration pursued a two-track diplomacy: agreements with the U.S.S.R. whenever possible and prevention of attempts by Russia to extend her influence into the third world. This denial of influence, now seen as guerrilla warfare consistent with Khrushchev's support on January 6, 1961, for "wars of liberation," was to be implemented by what Kennedy called "a wholly new kind of strategy, a wholly different kind of force and therefore a new and wholly different kind of military training." [6]

The technique of counterinsurgency was, of course, the "wholly different kind of force" that President Kennedy was contemplating. Concepts, such as "nation-building," aiding the poorer countries of the globe to reach what W. W. Rostow termed the "take-off stage," were created to align the desire for stability with that of containing communism, and so induced the seemingly paradoxical if not contradictory policy of assisting what Kennedy called "peaceful revolution." This Sisyphean task was far beyond the capabilities of the Kennedy administration, but the enormous strategic mobility that the United States possessed in the early 1960s so overshadowed Russia's capability that it seemed that the image of America as Atlas rather than as Sisyphus would prove more apt. Moreover, the abiding spirit of the Kennedy years was the desire to act. It seems now that energy was a quality judged in and for itself and as an apparently needed antidote to the inactivity and even lassitude of the Eisenhower era. In his concluding remarks on the Kennedy foreign policy, Anthony Hartley identifies the virus that infected that administration's conduct of foreign affairs: "not merely did [it] overestimate the difficulties of American power, but . . . it overestimated the difficulties of doing anything at all. . . . The Johnson era saw the dissolution of the Kennedy policy . . . above all, in its failure to stay within the modest bounds of reality."

The intellectual construction of trying to work out a harmonious relationship with the Soviet Union, combined with denying Russia influence in the third world, also displayed a genuine desire to remove tension between the two blocs. And the Johnson administration continued this policy. Continuity was the leitmotif of Johnson's program both in domestic and foreign affairs. Johnson's summit meeting with Soviet Premier Kosygin at Glassboro in 1967 did not conflict with the continued American build-up in Vietnam. Indeed, Russian mediation in the Vietnam conflict was sought again and again by President Johnson. Whether or not the Russians, in the light of the Sino–Soviet split, either could or would be able to influence Hanoi was another matter. But certainly American policymakers pursued the chimera of Russian mediation.

It has been said that had Kennedy lived, there would have been a de-escalation of the war in Vietnam. According to Kenneth O'Donnell, one of Kennedy's advisers, President Kennedy was only waiting until after the 1964 elections to pull out of Vietnam when the issue could not be used against him.[7]

Perhaps so. But we also have the testimony of a man who

was a principal foreign policy adviser to both Presidents Kennedy and Johnson. Walt Rostow has been emphatic in maintaining that Kennedy would have acted much as his successor did. In regard to intervention both in Southeast Asia and in the Dominican Republic in 1965, Rostow declares that Kennedy would have acted with equal toughness. In an interview in *The New York Times* (April 21, 1969), Rostow asserted that Kennedy intervened in Vietnam "because he said, 'I've got to hold Southeast Asia come hell or high water.'" Rostow also points out that Kennedy "made his flattest reaffirmation in 1963 of the 'domino theory'."

As far as using American forces to ensure a government friendly to the United States in the Dominican Republic, Rostow says:

I'll tell you one thing—I don't know if this is in the public record— but he [Kennedy] was determined that there would not be another Cuba. We had a small task force, of which I was a member, to find what would be the legal basis for using military power. That was Kennedy. . . . The problem is this. That the image they cooked up afterwards was cooked up by people who had very little to do with military and foreign policy. It was done basically for other purposes: to beat Johnson.

Such arguments of what President Kennedy would or would not have done had he lived are rather like the argument—"Would Keats have been a great poet had he not died so young?" A tragic death, hence the unfulfilled career of a promising man—be he statesman or poet—leaves us with only those fragments that he has shored against his ruins. That Kennedy increased our military commitment in Vietnam from a mere handful to approximately 16,000 military advisers is beyond dispute; that the White House at the very least encouraged the overthrow of South Vietnam's President Diem is also evident; that Kennedy in the wake of his disastrous meeting with Khrushchev in Vienna in 1961 felt it necessary to implement ever more quickly a strategy of flexible response is equally clear.

In its own way, however, the legacy of the Vietnam War finally became Johnson's war. The descent into the quagmire made it almost impossible to enunciate new policies, to move into the post-postwar world, and the tragic year of 1968—the year of assassins at home and the great Communist Tet offensive abroad—seemed finally to be an age which demanded a new image. And when the new President, Richard Nixon, declared that we were moving from "an era of confrontation" to one "of negotiation," he was at last spelling out the historic change which seemed both desirable and inevitable.

THREE

Though we have finally recognized the obsolescence of a worldview largely formulated to contain Communist territorial expansion, there is as yet no clearly defined American foreign policy as there was in the immediate postwar years —easy to sell to the Congress and the people. Rather, there have been the mere lineaments of a new policy, one which seeks to cope with a different world while creating a situation that remains ultimately advantageous to the United States. There is indeed a world elsewhere but, as we shall see, to discover this world requires the most skilled of navigators. For the hazardous creation of a new foreign policy we need not only the knowledge of past error and accomplishment but also the sense of, if not the exact bearings of, the landfall we are seeking.

Richard Nixon, who has promoted mere sufficiency of nuclear force with Russia during his administration, said the year he was elected, "I do not believe that the United States can afford to accept a concept of parity with the Soviet Union." He proclaimed that "the Nixon Doctrine says only that we will help those who help themselves," with the implication that the United States would withdraw from the Asian mainland. One week later (in July 1969) he said in Bangkok that "America will stand proudly with Thailand against those who might threaten it from abroad—or from within." [8] (Shades of the Eisenhower Doctrine!) Not only did Nixon reverse his policy toward China but he seemed even willing to fulfill the dire consequences of which he once warned. During the famous debates with John F. Kennedy in 1960, Nixon cautioned that admitting China to the United Nations "would give respectability to the communist regime which could immensely increase its power and prestige in Asia, and probably irreparably weaken the non-communist governments in the area." This is a roughly accurate statement of what is likely to occur.

How then can we explain Nixon's reversals of posture and policy once he was elected President? Did he come to the office with no worldview? Should he be seen as a mere opportunist? For those who have viewed him most critically, as Garry Wills once wrote, "There is one Nixon only, though there seem to be new ones all the time—he will try to be what people want." [9] A more sympathetic observer, such as French political analyst Pierre Hassner, describes him as a "pragmatic conservative." Whatever he has been called, Nixon revealed himself as President as a man who had begun to formulate an overall foreign policy sharply at variance with the dominant American postwar vision of the world, a vision which he himself once shared.

In part, Nixon learned from his years as a protégé of Dwight Eisenhower to be skeptical of purely military solutions, and he certainly embraced the concepts of Henry Kissinger, once the foreign policy adviser of the man who was his archrival, Nelson Rockefeller. But a major key to Nixon's philosophy in foreign affairs was his link with General de Gaulle. It is this bond which best helps us understand a man whose response to the highest office of this land was not unlike that of the towering figure from another age who befriended him when his political career was at its nadir and provided him with a model of greatness.

In asking for support for his New Economic Policy in September 1971, the President concluded his appeal to Congress by citing and then paraphrasing General de Gaulle: "America can be her true self only when she is engaged in a great enterprise." The echo of de Gaulle's memoirs was deliberate, for in his mature years Nixon had become an avid admirer of the General. And, on those occasions when the President startled the nation with a sudden reversal of policy, the General's admonition that "once action starts, criticism disappears" seemed particularly apt. Both the tactic and the rationale were Gaullist. Ruse, cunning, surprise—de Gaulle used all these in order to advance the vision of restoring France to the first rank. Unexpected tactics were necessary for the Machiavelli, so that Saint Joan might conquer.

It is of fundamental importance to realize that Nixon often consciously tried to imitate de Gaulle and that he wants history to view him the way history will view de Gaulle. De Gaulle wrote of "the contrast between inner power and outward control from which ascendancy is gained, just as style in a gambler consists in his ability to show greater coolness than usual when he has raised his stake." In a similar vein, Nixon once wrote: "The ability to be cool, confident and decisive in a crisis is not an inherited characteristic, but is the direct result of how well the individual has prepared himself for battle." It is amusing that General de Gaulle, the theorist of modern tank warfare, took his example from the game of poker, while Richard Nixon, an enthusiastic and successful poker player, chose the battlefield metaphor.

Nixon, like de Gaulle, was a man whose career seemed to be finished. In 1953, when de Gaulle was brooding alone at his country estate at Colombey, who would have predicted his return to power five years later? Who in 1962, when Nixon lost the governorship of California to Pat Brown, would have predicted his election as President of the United States only six years later?

Yet, when Nixon was out of office, de Gaulle treated him courteously; he spoke of Nixon as someone who should not be counted out, and seemed to agree that Nixon might, in some respects, be able to pattern himself after de Gaulle. Upon Nixon's election, almost the first order of business of the new President was to pay a visit to the French leader; moreover, Nixon's foreign policy adviser, Kissinger, shared both Nixon's admiration for de Gaulle and his desire to repair the fabric of Franco–American relations. It was on the 1969 visit to de Gaulle, according to C. L. Sulzberger, that the General told Nixon that "it was easier for the United States to leave Vietnam than it had been for France to leave

Algeria with its large French population." Nixon agreed and said that had he been in de Gaulle's position during the Algerian crisis, he would "probably have done the same thing." He also told the General that he would get out of Vietnam, "come what may." [10]

They made a curious pair, Charles de Gaulle and Richard Nixon, both of them profoundly shy human beings, the Frenchman cloaking himself in cynicism and elegance, the American in earnest moralism. Both employed a rhetoric of the past. In de Gaulle's case, his cynical tactical methods, combined with his vision of France's global role, enabled him to achieve a new reality by asserting France's independence from the two superpowers.

In Richard Nixon's case, greater strength than France possessed was used to try to establish a global balance of power which the White House believed only America could successfully engineer.

FOUR

There have always been two dominant strands among those seeking an international order in the postwar world. They are most easily defined in European terms and can be roughly divided into the Gaullist and the Monnetist camps. The Gaullist view, stressing what Stanley Hoffmann, Harvard professor of government, has called "the new legitimacy of the nation-state," believes in the viability of the nation as a major actor on the world's stage. Big powers such as the United States and the Soviet Union thus take their places as matinee idols, upon whose leading roles in shaping the future the peace of the world depends. Another group of policymakers believes that the day of the nation-state is drawing to a close; transnational forces will combine to create a more centralized international system. They derive much of their inspiration from de Gaulle's great opponent, Jean Monnet, who saw economics and technology as leading to a political federation of Western Europe. Their version of the Monnetist dream is that of a community of advanced, industrialized, non-Communist nations. As one of their most articulate spokesmen, Zbigniew Brzezinski of Columbia, put it: "The emergence of a community of the developed nations must still remain the central goal of United States policy."

Such a community would presumably stretch from Japan to Scandinavia, with the United States as its centerpiece, and would be a kind of model of the Atlanticist "grand design" of the Eisenhower-Kennedy eras. Moreover, in this federalist view, the community could be the beginning of a new international system that would be better able to cope with such problems as monetary stability, trade barriers, pollution, and population control—problems that would seem to transcend the ability of the nation-state, no matter what its size, to solve alone. This community would presumably develop joint policies toward the poorer countries of the globe and hold open the possibility of membership for Communist nations.

As Brzezinski has further argued: "Shared political values as well as economic progress clearly dictate the desirability of transforming the existing cooperation between Europe, Japan, and America into a more binding community of the developed nations. Failure to do so would be very costly for the future of mankind. At this stage of history only these three major units have the potential for developing truly cooperative relations, and this opportunity should not be forfeited. To argue the above is not to advocate the continuation of the cold war." [11]

Hoffmann, while fully aware of both chessboards—that of inter-state rivalry and that of transnational forces which gravely limit the autonomy of the nation-state—raises serious questions as to the ways by which "community-building" could be accomplished. "Should it," he asks, "be primarily the duty of the developed nations, as some advocate paternalistically? Can an international system as diverse as this one function effectively, without the active participation of all its members? . . . Can community-building proceed in such a way as not to seem a neo-colonial device through which the rich and the strong perpetuate their hold on the poor?" [12]

The great debate upon the future of American foreign policy, as we shall see, will focus in no small way on these two visions of the world which we have just delineated. Is it either possible or desirable to reconcile them? And what will be the consequences for both global and United States politics?

The world which President Nixon perceived conforms much more closely to the Gaullist model than to the Monnetist. His approach to world politics was to see a pattern of relationships involving five major power centers: the United States, Russia, China, Japan, and, eventually, Western Europe (including Britain, Ireland, Denmark, and Norway). In this pentagonal world each power center would be constrained by the others. Nixon first alluded to this concept in the summer of 1971 in Kansas City, when he explained the passing of the cold war. "Twenty-five years ago," he said, "we were number one in the world militarily, with no one who even challenged us, because we had a monopoly of atomic weapons. . . . Now, twenty-five years having passed . . . we see five great economic superpowers: the United States, Western Europe, the Soviet Union, China, and, of course, Japan."

Though it is palpably untrue that all five are "economic superpowers," Nixon's words revealed his consciousness of the pentagonal world he felt would be the next stage after the end of the cold war and the confrontation politics which characterized that period. Were he to have taken the older view—that the balance of power was simply a nuclear balance of terror between the United States and the Soviet Union—his rapprochement with China would not have been perceived by Moscow as a possible counterweight to Russia's global engagement.

FIVE

At the beginning of his electoral year, Nixon then articulated a concert of great powers that resembled in some respects the balance of power in Europe during much of the nineteenth century. "We must remember," he said, "the only time in the history of the world that we have had any extended periods of peace is when there has been a balance of power. It is when one nation becomes infinitely more powerful in relation to its potential competitor that the danger of war arises. . . . I think it will be a safer world and a better world if we have a strong, healthy United States, Europe, Soviet Union, China, Japan, each balancing the other, not playing one against the other, an even balance." [13]

In the search for a global balance of power, however, there are risks. For the nations that came together in Vienna after the generation of war that ended at Waterloo generally agreed on the desirability of such a balance among the five great powers in order to maintain the peace. Those who gathered at the Congress of Vienna in 1815— and, in particular, Metternich, Talleyrand and Castlereagh—understood the need to prevent any one power from becoming too dominant in Europe and thereby threatening the Continent with another war. Metternich, the great Austrian statesman who, in Henry Kissinger's words, became for the next generation the virtual "Prime Minister of Europe," laid down as an axiom of policy "the application of the principle of solidarity and equilibrium . . . and of the united efforts of states against the supremacy of one power." Russia, Prussia, Austria, France, and England—these were the five great powers of the post-Napoleonic world, and their achievement was to bring about a balance of power that was to give the world a century without a major war.

As Sir Harold Nicolson pointed out in his study of the Congress of Vienna: "It is thus a mistake to regard the balance of power as some iniquitous plotting of forces; it was rather the achievement of such a distribution of strength as would render aggression by any single country a policy of the greatest uncertainty and danger." The five European powers disagreed, however, about the extent to which they would act in concert to impose their will upon nations that were infected by the revolutionary virus that could destroy the established order. It was a static world, based upon the sacred principle of legitimacy, that they sought.

Those statesmen who gathered at Vienna were essentially men of the eighteenth century. They had learned to play the game of nations at a time when the concept of the balance of power had been refined to a certain degree of amorality that allowed for shifting alignments, sometimes with startling frequency. It was, as Hans Morgenthau has said, "the golden age of the balance of power in theory as well as practice." [14] Frederick the Great could not have put it more aptly when he wrote that "when the policy and the prudence of the princes of Europe lost sight of the maintenance of a just balance among the dominant powers, the constitution of the whole body politic resents it." Such a condition results in "disorder and confusion," and carries with it the danger of "the most disastrous revolutions." [15] The idea of the balance of power indeed derives from the eighteenth-century image of the divine clockmaker whose pendulum must swing at just the right measure.

What is especially significant about the balance of power as it developed after 1815 was its extension from the confines of Europe to a global system. As Morgenthau has pointed out, this transformation was clearly envisaged by the British Foreign Secretary George Canning (without whose support the Monroe Doctrine of 1823 could not have been effectuated), when he explained why Britain had not fought France to restore the balance of power after the French invasion of Spain. To defend his position Canning constructed a new balance of power through British recognition of the newly independent Latin American republics as a vital new element in the balance. It is worth quoting from Canning's great speech of December 12, 1826, before the House of Commons, for the concept is with us still in yet a new guise.

Is the balance of power a fixed and unalterable standard? Or is it not a standard perpetually varying, as civilization advances, and as new nations spring up, and take their place among established political communities? . . . If France occupied Spain, was it necessary, in order to avoid the consequences of that operation—that we should blockade Cadiz? No. I looked for another way—I saw materials for compensation in another hemisphere. Contemplating Spain, such as our ancestors had known her, I resolved that if France had Spain, it should not be Spain "with the Indies." I called the New World into existence, to redress the balance of the Old.

Today, Nixon might be said to have recognized the status of China as a great power in order to counteract the growing power of the Soviet Union.

The static equilibrium which was set up in Vienna in 1815 could not last: Canning foresaw this, and his successor Palmerston further undermined the Congress system by withdrawing Britain wholly from the ideological bonds that tied together the other four to England. The Vienna conference had as its aim the containment of a new Napoleonic Empire, or indeed, any nation which sought overweening power. But England did not intend intervention into the internal affairs of other nations solely in order to maintain the principle of absolute monarchy. In short, the principle of legitimacy, the maintenance of the status quo, which could be agreed upon in 1815 by all five powers, no longer meant the same thing to all five a decade later. What this did, however, was to put England in the position of being the holder of the balance. The concept of a balance of power as embodied in the Congress system—the first large-scale exercise of what is now called "summitry"—survived.

The Vienna conclave was unique in modern history—so

many statesmen gathered in one place to decide upon so many great events. Metternich himself recognized how unusual was this particular exercise in summit diplomacy. As he put it with no small degree of self-satisfaction: "As the sovereigns of Europe and their ministers met personally on the same spot, their diplomatic practices had to be adapted to the circumstances. The most difficult affairs, the most complicated questions are handled somehow from one room to another; no couriers, no exchanges of written notes, and no intermediaries between courts. All the inevitable delays have disappeared with the distances. Many affairs, which in other circumstances could not have been treated but slowly, were straightened out in a morning."

Thus, Canning's belief that international government by Congress had ended after Britain's defection from the policies of the other four in 1822 was not quite accurate. The Congress of Berlin in 1878, the Conference at Versailles in 1919, Yalta, Potsdam—all attest to the seduction of the Congress system. The failure of the Paris summit of Eisenhower, Khrushchev, Macmillan, and de Gaulle in 1960 is not likely to deter heads of states from meeting in other than bilateral sessions, as has been the style since the Paris debacle. If there emerges a pentagonal world which the United States now sees as both extant and desirable, then a congress of five powers is not the wholly remote possiblity that it seemed in the dark days of the cold war.

But it is important to recognize how the balance of power changed during the nineteenth century. And its change was due in no small part to the genius of the German Chancellor Otto von Bismarck, who saw the balance of power as essentially dynamic rather than static. Not a man born under the anciens régimes of the eighteenth century, and thus as

Talleyrand would have put it, "unable to know the sweetness of life," Bismarck did not cling to the status quo, the sacred principle of legitimacy which had been the previous cornerstone of Prussian foreign policy.

There is no better way to penetrate Bismarck's understanding of the new concept of the balance of power than by reading Nixon's foreign policy adviser Henry Kissinger's seminal essay on the man whom Kissinger termed "the white revolutionary." It has always been difficult to know where Nixon began and Kissinger left off. Or maybe it was simply the marriage of true minds: in any case, the fact that Kissinger should be the author of a book on Metternich and a study of Bismarck makes it imperative to understand Kissinger's perceptions of power and equilibrium in order to penetrate the new American foreign policy that emerged under the Nixon administration.

What Bismarck did was to challenge the very core of the international system as it had been devised by those statesmen who adapted the ancien régime's concept of the balance in order to remove temptation for conquest or domination, especially by France. Bismarck, forty years later, in his historic mission to unify Germany under the aegis of Prussia, no longer felt constrained to maintain the equilibrium set up by an earlier generation. For such a balance as existed after 1815 precluded the unification of Germany, and made the Holy Alliance of Prussia, Austria, and Russia an ideological alliance designed primarily to eradicate the virus of revolution, thus maintaining the legitimacy of absolute monarchy. By the 1830s, both France and England, the other members of the Concert of Europe, were too liberal to implement such a policy. But to Bismarck, ideology was foolish. Policy was "the art of the possible."

The idea that Prussia should separate herself from Austria, or indeed even contemplate an alliance with the "revolutionary" France of Napoleon III was an anathema to the political mentors of Bismarck. Yet Bismarck actually advocated a Prussian attack on Austria in order to improve Prussia's position. As Kissinger wrote: "Even in the heyday of the Metternich system, it was not unusual for a state to seek to improve its position; but every effort was made to endow change with the legitimacy of a European consensus. Pressures for change without even lip service to existing treaty relationships or to the Concert of Europe involved a revolution in prevailing diplomatic method. . . . Bismarck represented a new age. Equilibrium was seen not as harmony and mechanical balance, but as a statistical balance of forces in flux." [16]

Kissinger quotes at some length Bismarck's exchange of letters with his old mentor, Gerlach, a man who had grown up during the wars of the French Revolution, and who saw in Bismarck's opportunism a betrayal of ideological principles. For Bismarck power provided its own legitimacy. What shocked Gerlach was Bismarck's easy contemplation of an alliance with France, for in Bismarck's view all beliefs were valid. However, as Kissinger rightly stresses, "because of his magnificent grasp of the nuances of power relationships, Bismarck saw in his philosophy a doctrine of self-limitation." The trouble was that Bismarck was his own man: he could have no true successor. His greatness consisted not in having some master plan, a clear conceptual framework as did Metternich, but in the subtle methods by which he aligned his policies to changing circumstances. But as Kissinger concludes, "in the hands of others lacking his subtle touch, his methods led to the collapse of the nineteenth century state system. The nemesis of power is that, except in the hands of a master, reliance on it is more likely to produce a contest of arms than of self-restraint."

There is, of course, a crucial difference between the balance of power sought in the nineteenth century and such an order in the contemporary world. For the five major power centers today do not agree that such a global balance is even a desideratum. Moreover, any analogy between the Nixon-Kissinger game and the nineteenth-century balance would resemble the Bismarckian more than the Metternichian model. Our desire to improve relations with our ideological rivals is meant to be compatible with changing relationships with old allies, and indeed a position within the global balance ultimately favorable to us. During the forty years of peace that followed the Congress of Vienna, the great powers feared revolution. During the forty years of peace that followed the Franco–Prussian War they were afraid of each other. And so, as the British historian L. C. B. Seaman has pointed out: "What Bismarck bequeathed to Europe was not balance but extreme tension." [17]

Despite the changing nature of nineteenth-century European state relations, there *was* a Concert of Europe that tried, first with general consent, later within a framework of tension and secret alliances, to maintain equilibrium; the great global powers today are not capable as yet of operating together; a balance of power will exist only insofar as the powers act to constrain the overweening aspirations of any one power. And there is no guarantee that this will occur.

"Part of the reason for our difficulties," Kissinger once wrote, "is our reluctance to think in terms of power and equilibrium." He went on to criticize the American tendency to feel that "while other nations have interests, we have responsibilities; while other nations are concerned with equilibrium, we are concerned with the legal requirements of peace." [18]

As Talleyrand in his way and Bismarck in his would have urged in the last century, and as de Gaulle would have advised in turn, Nixon and Kissinger pursued a quest for equilibrium in a world in which they saw the nation-state as the most important force to be reckoned with.

NOTES

1. Richard Lowenthal, "A World Adrift," *Encounter*, February 1972, p. 23.

2. George Kennan, *Memoirs, 1925–1950*. Boston: Little, Brown, 1967. (Bantam Books), pp. 378 ff.

3. Anthony Hartley, "John Kennedy's Foreign Policy," *Foreign Policy*, No. 4, 1971, p. 78.

4. Anthony Hartley, "From World Policeman to Fortress America," *Moderne Welt*, Cologne, 1970, p. 150.

5. Richard Rovere, "Eisenhower Revisited—A Political Genius? A Brilliant Man?" *New York Times Magazine*, February 7, 1971, p. 58.

6. President Kennedy's speech at West Point, June 6, 1962. Quoted by Hartley in "John Kennedy's Foreign Policy," p. 81.

7. Kenneth O'Donnell, "L.B.J. and the Kennedys," *Life* Magazine, August 7, 1970, p. 51.

8. See *The New York Times*, July 31, 1969.

9. Garry Wills, *Nixon Agonistes*. Boston: Houghton Mifflin, 1970, p. 406.

10. Ross Terrill, *The 800,000,000*. Boston: Atlantic-Little, Brown, 1972, p. 145.

11. Zbigniew Brzezinski, "The Balance of Power," *Foreign Policy*, No. 7, 1972, p. 59.

12. Stanley Hoffmann, "Weighing the Balance of Power," *Foreign Affairs*, July 1972, p. 636.

13. Interview in *Time* Magazine, January 3, 1972, p. 15.

14. Hans Morgenthau, *Politics Among Nations*. 4th ed. New York: Alfred A. Knopf, 1968, p. 183.

15. Quoted by Morgenthau in *Politics Among Nations*, p. 183.

16. Henry Kissinger, "Bismarck: The White Revolutionary," *Daedalus*, Summer 1968, p. 909.

17. L.C.B. Seaman, *From Vienna to Versailles*. London: Methuen, 1955, p. 130.

18. Henry Kissinger, "Central Issues of American Foreign Policy," *Agenda for the Nation*. Washington, D.C.: The Brookings Institution, 1968, p. 610.

II

BALANCING THE POWERS

We have learnt that all extensions of territory, all usurpations, by force or by fraud, which have been connected by prejudice with the idea of "rank," of "hegemony," of "political stability," of "superiority" in the order of the Powers, are only cruel jests of political lunacy, false estimates of power, and that their real effect is to increase the difficulty of administration and to diminish the happiness and security of the governed for the passing interest or for the vanity of those who govern.

*—T*ALLEYRAND

ONE

When the need for a balance of power extended beyond the confines of Europe, the equilibrium sought became even more difficult to attain. By the latter half of the nineteenth century, territorial settlements in the form of colonies largely replaced the cutting up of the map of Europe. But by Versailles, even colonization no longer seemed an appropriate method of compensation. Europe again became the foreground of territorial compensation as a means of re-establishing the balance, though the compensations were designed under the more benevolent-seeming schema of self-determination. The League of Nations was to be the permanent form of international government that would, under a different rubric, finally enshrine the congress system. It would also, it was supposed, replace the iniquitous balance-of-power system Woodrow Wilson so despised. Agreements, such as Locarno (1925) that then led to the Briand-Kellogg Peace Pact (1928) to outlaw war, were further attempts to guarantee by something other than the classic balance of power the peace and security of Europe.

During the same period of *entre deux guerres,* the global balance outside Europe that had been set up prior to 1914 remained more or less intact until Germany, Italy, and Japan decided to extend their hegemonies. Moreover, the United States may have been "isolationist" as far as Europe was concerned but not in Latin America where intervention was still a fact of life, continuing in the 1920s to reflect Theodore Roosevelt's Secretary of State Root's declaration that the

United States was "sovereign upon this continent, and that its fiat is law." Much of the global map remained colored red and green as the British and French Empires made sure that, at least outside Europe, *their* fiat would also remain law.

To attempt to restore a global balance of power after the wreckage of the international system during World War II and its quarter-century aftermath, the post-cold war period required not only a conceptual basis which both Nixon and Kissinger developed; it also required a contemporary methodology. In the early months of the Nixon administration, the theory of "linkage" was expounded. This concept stressed the interrelationship of the United States and the Soviet Union on a global level. For example, negotiations with Moscow on the Middle East would presumably affect Soviet behavior in other places such as Berlin or in the Strategic Arms Limitation Talks (SALT), and, with any luck at all, in Hanoi. Things did not work out quite that neatly, however. There was a very big question of whether the Soviet Union could deliver: doubtful indeed in Hanoi and even more questionable in Cairo. By the same token, neither was Washington able to deliver in Jerusalem, and Moscow might well question America's influence upon Seoul—or even Saigon.

Even had the theory been soundly based, the constraints on the power of the Soviet Union are considerable, just as they are upon the United States. It was precisely the difficulty of operating within such a schematic framework that led the Nixon administration to drop its emphasis on linkage and to concentrate on specific areas where agreements could be reached. Thus, parallel progress could be made in Central Europe with the Four-Power Berlin Agreement of

1972 tied to the West German–Soviet 1970 treaty renouncing the use of force and the 1970 pact confirming the frontiers between Poland and Germany.

Any rapprochement between America and Russia—as between Washington and Peking—would certainly influence the decisions taken by smaller, so-called nonaligned nations. But, for example, the expulsion of Russian military advisers from Egypt in 1972 did not really result from any concept of linkage. At the same time, Cairo could hardly be expected to rejoice at warmer American–Soviet relations, and its reaction to the changed climate may have affected its contacts with the Russians. In any event both Washington and Moscow were apparently surprised.

TWO

Just as linkage at first seemed to provide the methodology by which equilibrium could be pursued, the self-styled Nixon Doctrine was to provide the military-strategic rationale by which the United States could implement its diplomacy. It had already become the conventional wisdom by the end of the Johnson administration that the United States neither could nor should be the "world's policeman." The Nixon Doctrine appeared on the surface to be a translation of this mood and maxim into a national policy: but on closer examination the Doctrine proved deeply ambiguous. In its starkest form "the Nixon Doctrine says only that we will help those who help themselves." This was President Nixon's own formulation, for Henry Kissinger allegedly said: "It's his doctrine, and he can damned well do what he wants with it."

The ambiguity of the Doctrine lies in its insistence that America maintain her global commitments but with reduced military capacities. To refuse to be the world's policeman implies, at the very least, a policy of disengagement. How then can the maintenance of our existing commitments be consistent with a policy of worldwide disengagement? This is the heart of the matter, and is to be found within the logical contradiction between objectives and strategy. Essentially, as defense specialist Earl C. Ravenal has written, "we are to support the same level of potential involvement with smaller conventional forces." Moreover, "the specter of intervention will remain, but the risk of defeat or stalemate will be greater; or the nuclear threshold will be lower. The fundamental issues of interests, commitments and alliances are not resolved." [1]

Nixon himself explained his own rationale as a response to the desire of the Kennedy–Johnson administrations for a global gendarmerie:

The stated basis of our conventional posture in the 1960s was the so-called "2½ war" principle. According to it, United States forces would be maintained for a three-month conventional forward defense of NATO, a defense of Korea or Southeast Asia against a full-scale Chinese attack, and a minor contingency—all simultaneously. These force levels were never reached.

In the effort to harmonize doctrine and capability, we chose what is best described as the "1½ war" strategy. Under it we will maintain in peacetime general purpose forces adequate for simultaneously meeting a major Communist attack in either Europe or Asia, assisting allies against non-Chinese threats in Asia, and contending with a contingency elsewhere. [2]

This does not mean that the Nixon Doctrine would necessarily force an escalation from conventional to nuclear war. Nor was it intended to point in this direction. But, as Ravenal stresses, "the $1\frac{1}{2}$ war strategy provided the President with fewer alternatives, and so renders the resort to nuclear weapons a more compelling choice, as well as making nuclear threat a more obvious residual feature of our diplomacy."

In fact, rather than a return to the doctrine of "massive retaliation" and its implied protection of newly acquired client-states as was the major defense posture of the 1950s, the Doctrine really depends for its true rationale on the reliance upon foreign military forces. American military assistance will buttress such forces and so help the United States to bridge the gap between its objectives and its military capabilities.

Such reliance—as Vietnamization showed—proves highly dubious. If a client-state cannot, as Nixon himself put it, "hack it," the resort to nuclear weapons becomes tempting. Nixon himself, rejecting the use of "massive retaliation," employed the terms "realistic deterrence" and "*truly* flexible response," an implied criticism of the military doctrine of the 1960s.

But what do these phrases really portend? How are the contradictions to be reconciled? Such language was largely used to gloss over the essential reality and the essential contradiction: the reality is the scaling down of direct American military involvement on a global scale; the contradiction, the continuance of commitments. The resolution lies in the agreements sought between the United States and its main adversaries—Russia and China—that would allow

the commitments to be unimplemented if not wholly abandoned. Thus, the rhetoric of disengagement employed by
President Nixon was a dangerous one. When the United
States failed to impose its solution on Indochina, America
did not become "a pitiful, helpless giant," any more than
did the Soviet Union when it overextended itself by placing
missiles in Cuba.

The act of disengagement—the act that Canning practiced with such consummate mastery a century ago—depends in no small degree on the correct use of language.
Though one's utterances may be Delphic at times, as were
de Gaulle's, they must never be so hyperbolic or so misleading that the actual policy one might choose to follow becomes perverted. Ravenal, in his analysis of the Nixon Doctrine, poses the question of whether the future for American
foreign policy will be neo-imperial or post-imperial. To discover that answer and so to chart the future is to define the
method of disengagement that the United States must follow if it is to secure for itself what Jefferson demanded of us
—that we "may not advance beyond safe measures of
power, that a salutary balance may be ever maintained
among nations and that our peace, commerce, and friendship may be sought and cultivated by all."

THREE

The "salutary balance" that the Nixon-Kissinger policy
sought relied on linkage of major and minor issues between
the superpowers; it relied on the substitution of foreign
forces for American troops; and it sought a "low profile" by

maintaining that people should not pay attention to what the administration said but rather to what it did.

But it should not be supposed that a five-power world and the balance of power necessarily imply a policy of "spheres of influence." Though the great powers will always try to ensure that the countries bordering them are not hostile—and to this extent certainly seek spheres of influence, as in Eastern Europe and the Caribbean—the competition among them in other parts of the world might well be for access and influence rather than for hegemony.[3]

If the great powers, in concert or individually, constrain one another, they are likely to find themselves increasingly excluded from spheres of influence. Even in Eastern Europe, Rumania enjoys a large measure of independence. Cuba has successfully resisted the United States. And one purpose of the American rapprochement with China was to counter a Russian sphere in South Asia.

A spheres-of-influence policy would not necessarily be a bad idea if it were workable. But herein lies the central question: is such a policy either possible or desirable? Is it more or less likely to lead to conflict? The unlikelihood of such agreement among the great powers is the primary reason why the evolution of such a policy is so dubious. Ronald Steel, forcefully making a case for a spheres-of-influence policy, writes that "a true balance of power must be based on spheres of influence, which grant to the great powers certain rights in areas they deem essential to their own security."[4] He calls this a "mature" spheres-of-influence policy because "to rule out intervention outside the sphere of influence is not to justify it within the sphere." He would not allow the great powers "carte blanche to threaten those areas as colonies."

In refuting Steel's argument, Earl Ravenal has argued that Steel "identifies neither the guarantor of this constraint nor the means that such a guarantor might apply without breaching his stricture of non-intervention." [5] Indeed, Steel himself recognizes that "perhaps the best way to avoid such dominance by a single hegemonic power is the creation of several power centers," i.e., a balance of power. But it is less likely that the great powers will conspire to constrain hegemonic ambitions within any so-called sphere of influence than that the countries themselves within such a "sphere"— local and regional forces—will resist mightily the ambitions of any power to stake out such an area as its own. In Eastern Europe, we have already witnessed time and again the resistance to Russian hegemony over the region: in Yugoslavia immediately after World War II, in Poland and Hungary in 1956, in Czechoslovakia in 1968, in Rumania throughout the 1960s. In Latin America, a presumed United States sphere, Cuba, Chile, and Peru, in varying degrees, have strongly and successfully reduced American hegemonic ambitions. The invasion of Santo Domingo in 1964 may have marked the last time the United States intervenes militarily in the affairs of Latin American states; the same may be true of the Soviet Union's intervention in Czechoslovakia in 1968. Finally, it is difficult to believe that Vietnam will not resist any hegemonic ambitions of China as she has for centuries. The same could be said of India vis-à-vis the Soviet Union.

The real danger in even attempting to contest a sphere of influence has been seen most forcefully in the Middle East. It is precisely in such a gray area that the great powers appear to see their contest as one not directed openly at one another but, as it were, played out for a sphere of influence that would be acknowledged by the other. Thus, the probability of conflict is greatest at the very edges of the so-called spheres, for such spheres are not drawn by a compass upon the abstract map of the globe. They are fuzzy and ill-defined, both by those who might desire them and by those nations, both large and small, that would resist them.

The Middle East also remains a good example of an area where neither the United States nor the Soviet Union has been able to establish a true sphere of influence; nor is either one very likely to in the near future. But in their jockeying for positions in this volatile region both great powers could easily find themselves inheriting or being perceived as the inheritors of such spheres. In a perceptive analysis of the relations between the West and the Middle East, John C. Campbell and Helen Caruso state that in the 1970s the question is no longer "how to exclude any Soviet presence but how to adjust to it" so that the Western non-Communist nations would have access to the area.[6] In fact, as Campbell and Caruso are careful to emphasize, the Russian presence does not "put the Middle East in a Soviet sphere of influence." By the same token, despite both Soviet and Arab accusations, Israel, while dependent on the United States for arms, is also not within an American sphere. The inability of Washington to influence Israel's policies since the Six-Day War of 1967 bears grim testimony to the falsity of this notion.

Yet the Nixon administration's numerous statements that it would not allow the balance to be tilted against Israel seemed to confirm the fact that America was committed to the Israelis and the U.S.S.R. committed to the other side. The real need in the Middle East is not to seek spheres of influence but to establish a stable regional balance of power. The danger of a local conflict which neither Washington nor Moscow could control should point up the desirability of seeking some arrangement to keep open the principles of access and influence; thus if competition must continue, let it at least be confined to the political arena. If any region could profit from equilibrium and one which need not exclude Europe, Japan, or even China—it is the Middle East.

FOUR

The difficulty of playing great-power politics to contain conflict and establish a balance of power was demonstrated most graphically by the interplay of Russia, America, and China in the conflict over Bangladesh. As did de Gaulle in his assessment of France's role in the Israeli–Arab conflict, so, too, did Nixon mistake the situation in South Asia; and with much the same result. Both countries would have preferred that such a conflict not take place. Both countries would have been wiser to remain completely neutral in the event of an attack. Neither really did so. Both lost influence to the Soviet Union.

By aligning itself with China, the United States tried to create a situation in which India, despite its new twenty-year friendship pact with the U.S.S.R., would be so intimidated as to avoid military operations against Pakistan. (In fact, the pact was directed as much against China as it was against Pakistan, and gave India some insurance against the new United States–China rapprochement.) But neither Peking nor Washington was prepared to make its threats effective. For the United States, domestic constraints against its involvement in Asia prevented any substantial American engagement, either of men or materiel. China, though free from domestic limitations, was constrained by her own strategic problems. Fearful of Russian advances along her own border, her military leadership weakened after the recent purge, China was wary of putting any direct military pressure on India; thus, Peking was left to fulminate in the United Nations against Russian ambitions. Only Russia had neither domestic constraints nor shortage of weaponry.

Once it became clear that India had indeed attacked, and that Russia would fully support India's course, Washington let it be known that such behavior would jeopardize the scheduled visit of President Nixon to the Soviet Union. But the threat lacked credibility; Nixon would have had to sacrifice, at least temporarily, a major objective—closer American–Soviet relations—for a relatively minor one: supporting a weak regional power. Moreover, Nixon had already stated that the United States accepted legitimate Chinese and Soviet interests in South Asia in order to create stability.[7] The effectiveness of the Indian attack, the weakness of Pakistan in the West—both also made ineffectual the administration's efforts to show its authority by sending warships into the Bay of Bengal.

From Pakistan's vantage point, relying on the great powers to balance off one another may have been the only choice she had. But it proved a poor one. Pakistan erred in evaluating the ability of either America or China to deliver the goods. The balance of power that had existed in some tentative form in South Asia prior to the Bangladesh upheaval and the Indo–Pak war was finally shattered. Russian preponderance is now evident to all. Misperceptions on the part of two of the great powers involved—America and China—resulted not in the success but the failure of the two powers to constrain the third.

In the resulting debacle the administration tried to make a case, ex post facto, for its role in preventing the war from widening and hence demonstrating that its balance-of-power politics were still in good working order. Washington claimed that it put sufficient pressure on the Russians so that the Indians were prevented from dismembering West Pakistan. In fact, Mrs. Gandhi probably had no intention of launching such an attack and being saddled with such a "victory." Asian specialist William J. Barnds questioned: "Even if India had been intent upon destroying West Pakistan, what concern was that of the [United States] if such areas were important chiefly as they affected relations among the major powers?" The answer is that, in the Nixon-Kissinger view of the world, "events in such areas as the subcontinent are *seen* as affecting relations between the major powers whenever these powers are on the opposite side of regional conflicts." [8]

Henry Kissinger made this view explicit when he asked rhetorically at a meeting of the National Security Council Action Group on December 8, 1971: "Can we allow a United States ally [i.e., Pakistan] to go down completely?" He projected the regional conflict onto a global scale by declaring that "what we may be witnessing is a situation wherein a country [India] equipped and supported by the Soviets, may be turning half of Pakistan into an impotent state and the other half into a vassal. We must consider what would be the impact of the current situation in the larger complex of world affairs." After this dire scenario, however, Kissinger added that Mrs. Gandhi "is cold blooded and will not turn India into a Soviet satellite merely because of pique." [9]

In fact, there was little the United States could have done to prevent closer ties between New Delhi and Moscow without jeopardizing its far more important démarche toward China. What it could have done was to abstain from any involvement in the Indo–Pak conflict. Only when the hollowness of its policy became evident to all did the administration seek to re-establish American access and influence in the region. Only by pursuing such a course can the United States enter into even such a tenuous balance-of-power situation as may once again exist in the subcontinent.

FIVE

Henry Kissinger, it was said, once remarked to a South American foreign minister that the true axis of United States foreign policy is a horizontal one, running from Moscow to Peking and passing through Bonn and Washington. And, indeed, it has been along this central strategic balance that the Nixon administration scored its most notable successes. Moreover, it is along this axis that balance-of-power politics has revealed both its limitations and its potential.

It was, of course, Nixon's visits to China and Russia that revealed most clearly the lines of this policy. In planning the China trip the old tie to de Gaulle was again evident. According to Ross Terrill, Nixon first let it be known that he would like to "normalize relations with China" when he saw de Gaulle in 1969.[10] The General passed this on to the

Chinese leaders who were avowed de Gaulle admirers. That initial contact, combined with the continued withdrawal of American troops from Southeast Asia, apparently convinced Peking that Nixon meant what he said.

The roots of Nixon's China policy, however, were certainly not evident during his years as Vice President when he seized on the so-called loss of China to the Communists by Truman and Acheson as a potent campaign issue with which to belabor the Democrats. On the other hand, it cannot be said to date solely from his post-election relationship with Henry Kissinger. A full year prior to the election in 1968, Nixon was writing in *Foreign Affairs*: "Taking the long view, we simply cannot afford to leave China forever outside the family of nations, there to nurture its fantasies, cherish its hates and threaten its neighbors. There is no place on this small planet for a billion of its potentially most able people to live in angry isolation." He went on to warn that "if our long-range aim is to pull China back into the family of nations, we must avoid the impression that the great powers or the European powers are 'ganging up'." This theme was continued after the election, in early December 1968, in a conversation with a British journalist. After repeating some of the points he had made in *Foreign Affairs*, Nixon concluded: "Thus our aim should be to persuade China . . . that its own national interest requires a turning away from foreign adventures and a turning inward toward the solution of its own domestic problems. Then, I believe, Communist China will begin to come to the conclusions the Soviet leaders came to several years ago. Then the dialogue with China can and should be opened."

The China policy is also another good illustration of the difficulty of knowing where Nixon began and Kissinger left

off, for Kissinger himself was saying in 1966 that "policy
could probably be altered much more dramatically in Communist China than in the more institutionalized Communist countries." [11] Certainly Nixon's belief that a conservative President has more freedom to pursue a radical policy
toward the Communists than a liberal was something the
young Nixon might have learned from Eisenhower, who ultimately settled for terms ending the Korean War that Truman had been unable to accept.

In his State of the World Message, issued just prior to his
China trip, the President suggested that Taipei and Peking
negotiate their differences. "The ultimate relationship between Taiwan and the mainland," he said, "is not a matter
for the United States to decide. A peaceful resolution of this
problem by the parties would do much to reduce tensions in
the Far East." Such a remark had been unprecedented
since 1949, when President Truman declared that Taiwan
was "China's internal affair." Kissinger was even more explicit at a press conference on November 30, 1971, when he
said: "Our position is that the ultimate disposition, the ultimate relationship of Taiwan to the People's Republic of
China, should be settled by direct negotiations between
Taiwan and the People's Republic of China."

What actually came out of the China visit was less explicit than even their statements indicated. The démarche
itself was a happening, the event itself more important as
symbolism. For at least on the diplomatic-strategic board
the triangular relationship of Russia, China, and America
has been visibly evident. And the consequences of this
three-power *ménage à trois* will have to be reckoned with for
some time to come. It is also worth noting that so important
were great power relations to both Peking and to Moscow

that Communist leaders in both countries received the American President, in the first instance after heavy bombing of North Vietnam had been resumed, and, in the second, after the mining of Haiphong harbor by American warplanes.

In fact, the Shanghai Communiqué of February 27, 1972, was somewhat cursory on the Taiwan question. Washington said that the United States "reaffirms its interest in a peaceful settlement of the Taiwan question by the Chinese themselves." Peking was more obdurate, as might be expected; the Chinese insisted that "the government of the People's Republic of China is the sole legal government of China" and that "Taiwan is a province of China," and finally, that "the liberation of Taiwan is China's internal affair in which no other country has the right to interfere."

What the United States has done in abandoning its rigid support of Taiwan has not only helped Washington re-establish communications with the mainland but also demonstrated that, despite the security pact the United States maintains with Taiwan, China's eastern border is secure.

More careful scrutiny should be paid to the joint affirmation of the five principles: "respect for the sovereignty and territorial integrity of all states; nonaggression against other states; noninterference in the internal affairs of other states; equality and mutual benefit; and peaceful coexistence."

There is an element of isolationism looked at from the vantage point of Peking. By insisting on the integrity of the nation-state in a so-called age of transnationalism, the Chinese demand ideological freedom, the license to support revolutions ("wars of liberation"), and to act as self-appointed spokesmen for the third world while protecting themselves from the encroachments of the Soviet Union and protecting their own continuing social revolution. All this, however, presumes that the Chinese are not imposing their own hegemonic ambitions upon others. From Washington's viewpoint the five principles are a reaffirmation of the end of a policy of confrontation, thus less concern with the internal character of the nation-state and more concern over the pattern of relationships based upon balance-of-power assumptions.

Both Peking and Washington explicitly opposed any nation's efforts to establish "hegemony in the Asia–Pacific region." Both America and China can invoke balance-of-power considerations in this respect, particularly with regard to any ambitions the Soviet Union might harbor in this area. Richard Nixon put it succinctly when he said: "We agreed that we are opposed to the domination of the Pacific area by any power." [12] China, however, to use Earl Ravenal's distinctions, "is an intra-regional power and invokes a distant power to avoid its own imminent subordination." America, on the other hand, "is an extra-regional power and calls forth an indigenous power to control the emergence of a . . . hypothetical challenge." [13]

Such considerations point up America's global engagement. Since only Russia and America can effectively challenge one another in any region of the world, Chou En-lai was probably fully aware of the absurdity of President Nixon's hyperbolic rhetoric when he toasted the Chinese Prime Minister at the farewell banquet in Shanghai with the words, "Our two peoples tonight hold the future of the world in our hands."

SIX

A statement of such magnitude would have been more appropriate if no less arrogant had it been directed to the Russians. The voyage to Moscow, most significantly, did result in concrete agreements. It was less an artistic *trompe l'oeil* than a coldly mirrored portrait of hard bargainers. And overarching both trips to the respective Communist capitals is the implicit guarantee that the United States has provided. In substance, America has assured the Russians that their western border will not be threatened just as China's apprehension over her eastern border has been eased. In this aspect of the balancing act among the three ideological antagonists, Washington can proclaim its neutrality in the event of any conflict between the two Communist powers while perhaps enjoying, or at least reaping, whatever benefits it can from the continuing tension between China and Russia.

Henry Kissinger articulated a somewhat similar view of the new triangular diplomacy with Moscow and Peking by stating just prior to the trip to Moscow: "We will not discuss one of them in the capital of the other. We recognize that they have serious differences with each other on a number of issues in which the United States is not primarily engaged—one of them being the border dispute, the other one being an ideological conflict over the interpretation of Leninist doctrine, with respect to which our competence is not universally recognized." [14]

What, then, were the summit accords of May 29, 1972?

There were three principles: peaceful coexistence (for which, read ideology subordinated to nationalistic consider- ations); great power restraint (such as will undoubtedly re- side in the eye of the beholder); and more summit meetings. In the communiqué more immediately significant results were apparent: that a European Security Conference should be convened "without undue delay"; the need for a "reciprocal" reduction of armed forces in Central Europe; that the United Nations representative should pursue fur- ther efforts to achieve a settlement in the Middle East; that increased trade is desirable; that each side set forth its posi- tion regarding Vietnam without vituperation. But by far the most important agreement struck in the Kremlin was the first accords deriving from the Strategic Arms Limita- tion Talks (SALT). The accords fell into two parts: (1) a treaty of unlimited duration on antiballistic missiles (ABMs), and (2) a five-year freeze on offensive strategic weapons.*

While such agreements are to be welcomed, the agree-

* More precisely, the treaty limits each nation to two ABM sites, one for the national capital and the other to protect one field of intercontinental ballistic missiles (ICBMs). Each site will consist of 100 ABMs, or a total of 200 for each country. The interim offensive agreement limits ICBMs to those under construction or deployed at the time of the signing of the treaty (May 26) or on July 1, 1972. This means about 1,600 ICBMs for the Soviet Union, including 300 large SS-9s, and 1,054 ICBMs for the United States, including 1,000 Minutemen and 54 Titans. It also freezes construction of submarine-launched ballistic missiles on all nuclear submarines at present levels.

ments are but a small beginning in any truly significant reduction of armaments by the two superpowers. Since the interim agreement on offensive weapons does not curb the
quality of the weapons involved, a larger defense expendi-
ture may be pressed by the military. An upgrading of
offensive nuclear weapons can continue as each superpower
adds more and more warheads to its existing stockpile. New
bombers, submarines, and other conventional weapons can
be—and undoubtedly will be—developed.

Pressures by the military in both the United States and
the Soviet Union to limit severely any meaningful arms
control agreements are, of course, to be expected. Both
Chou En-lai and Leonid Brezhnev could see their respective
positions undermined by those hardliners in the Party who
would be suspicious of any deals with the Americans. As Soviet expert Marshall Shulman has stressed, it took several
years, prior to the twenty-fourth Soviet Party Congress, held
in the spring of 1971, for Brezhnev to fully assert his control
over the course that was eventually followed. In Brezhnev's
view, pushing ahead on the economic front was paramount.
The Russian acquiescence in Brandt's Ostpolitik, the SALT
talks, the Nixon summit—the economic priority was central
to all such decisions.[15]

For the United States, to proceed to SALT II by stepping
up our offensive weapons program in order to have yet another "bargaining chip" to play off against the Russians virtually begs the question of the very meaning of arms control. If arms limitations are not pursued with the ultimate
aim of arms reduction, but rather as a means by which we
simply invent new deployments, then the equilibrium which
Nixon and Kissinger ostensibly seek will prove a hollow
joke indeed. Kissinger himself stated in the wake of the

Moscow arms agreements that "no nuclear agreement that brings disadvantages to either side can possibly last and can possibly bring about anything other than a new cycle of insecurity." He added that "in traditional diplomacy the aim was, through an accumulation of small advantages, to gain a qualitative edge over your major rivals. In the nuclear age, the most dangerous thing to aim for is a qualitative edge over your major rivals." [16]

Nevertheless, the trade-offs that any administration feels it must provide the Pentagon in order to pursue the foreign policy goals Kissinger apparently aimed for may prove so high as to vitiate his insights. For, as Shulman has pointed out in regard to the process used by Kennedy to obtain Senate support for the 1963 Partial Test-ban Treaty: "In that unfortunate case, such hostages were given in the form of assurances that underground testing would be greatly increased [so] that the net effect was to further stimulate the arms race."

Opening new trade channels, a key point of discussion between Brezhnev and Nixon, proved far more difficult than reaching even the limited arms-control agreements characterized by SALT I. However, the arms-control talks had been going on for nearly three years, and, even at that, agreements resulted only because of last-minute decisions made at the supreme level.

In his explanation of the Declaration of Principles that Kissinger gave at a press conference in Moscow (May 29, 1972), he stated that speculation "about the linkages between trade and other political problems happen[s] to be quite wrong." He denied explicitly that "we linked trade to Vietnam." An implicit linkage was another matter, since Kissinger went on to say that "it is correct that it has always been understood, which you could say about any one of these problems, that as our general relationships improve, we can accelerate progress in every area, but this is no more true of trade than anything else, and there was never any direct linkage."

Yet Secretary of Commerce Peterson, when questioned on May 28, 1972, on the possibility of a "very specific link" between Vietnam and trade, stressed the more subtle, implicit linkage between these two issues. He suggested that "both from talking to the President today and Henry Kissinger yesterday . . . the kind of linkage is not that kind of linkage, as in a chain, but rather a more general kind of linkage. In our country if we are going to expand credit terms . . . I think that if indeed the Vietnam situation were in more positive shape vis-à-vis the Soviets than it is now, that would be a helpful, positive factor." [17]

Whether, as I.F. Stone said, "the carrot of trade enabled Nixon to get away with the club of the blockade [of Haiphong]," was an accurate assessment of the tone of the Moscow discussions, the facts still remain irreducible. Linkage is—and will remain—a highly limited concept. The ability —even if there were the desire—of Russia to put pressure on Hanoi to end the war on terms relatively favorable to the United States was always virtually nil.

What is evident is that after two summit visits to the Rome and Byzantium of the Communist world, the fate of Indochina no longer can block the beginnings of a new relationship among the three powers. But Indochina—its settlement, its past, and its future—can affect profoundly the establishment of a new world order in which equilibrium, regional balances of power, and peaceful competition for access and influence become the dominant rules of the game on the strategic-political chessboard.

SEVEN

In Europe and Japan—the remaining elements in the pentagonal world in the making—one has, in the first instance, a power in concept only, and in the second, an economic power whose unwillingness to assume a military-political posture consonant with its economic strength has hobbled the notion of a proper Japanese role in a global power balance. The moves made by the Nixon administration, particularly the unilateral imposition of a 10 percent surcharge on imports in August 1971, not only raised the specter of protectionism, but also provided a further push toward the assertion of nationalism by these other two power centers. The aim of Nixon's New Economic Policy (his NEP with its ironic Leninist initials) was, in part, to rectify the American imbalance of payments by demanding that the other rich nations re-value their currency upwards; this, along with a disposition to end dependency on the dollar to finance world trade, had great merit.

But the public manner with which the then Secretary of the Treasury John Connally explained the reasons for United States actions was both arrogant and fatuous. "We had a problem," he said in Britain at the meeting of the finance ministers of the leading economic powers, "and we're sharing it with the world, just like we shared our prosperity." Such a remark undermines what were the real goals of the Secretary, namely, to force a recasting of the international monetary system by talking tough abroad in order to wring from Congress concessions that would normally be hard to obtain. Moreover, as the Europeans and Japanese well knew, it was the costs of the Indochina War and the unwillingness—particularly of President Johnson— to explain honestly the price of such a war that had been at the core of the American balance-of-payments problems. Such statements as these, including the theatricality of the announcement of the trip to China without bothering to consult with the Japanese beforehand—while these moves are often applauded by the electorate at home, they also set dangerous precedents for the future.

Toward Europe, with which we have the strongest ties, American policy has become less predictable. European policy, on the other hand, is trying to readjust to the changed world when Atlanticism—the two-pillar system by which the United States and Western Europe were to confront the Soviet colossus—is no longer the main thrust of American policy. How does this "European Europe," which de Gaulle extolled as the apotheosis of the new nation-state, fit into a schema that is called a pentagonal world?

To say that there is no Europe begs the question: there *is* a Europe in the making. The admittance of Great Britain, Ireland, Denmark, and even a Norway into the European Community would create a grouping of 250 million people, with a gross national product of $500 million. It would be the greatest trading bloc in the world; it would be the second richest economic power after the United States. And it would have a larger population than either America or Russia. Already Europe has begun, however hesitantly, to formulate some common foreign policy positions. The summit meeting in the fall of 1972 in Paris, the Davignon Report setting forth the need for periodic consultations on foreign policy at the ministerial level, some meetings on problems in the Middle East, certain joint ventures (not overly successful) on the construction of military aircraft and weaponry, the proposed political secretariat—all are signs of eventual cohesion.

Though Europe's first priorities will be to align economic and monetary policies, political and military policies will follow, and perhaps in some case precede the technocracy of economics. Political considerations—any more than economic—cannot be postponed, precisely because the United States has moved into a new era in its own relations with the Communist powers. The fact of proposed American troop withdrawals from Europe more than the exact numbers involved poses irreducible questions for the Europeans. It may well be that such troop withdrawals will be tied to negotiations with the Soviets on the basis of mutual and balanced force reductions. Moreover, Russian concessions in this area are now likely, despite the stresses that continue in Eastern Europe. The American rapprochement with China makes it all the more important for Russia to gain such guarantees in Central Europe to allow her to concentrate the thrust of her forces toward the East. Indeed, Russia since the downfall of Khrushchev has been expanding as a global superpower, no longer content with merely nuclear strength. For the Russians, at least, Mahan's doctrines are not forgotten.

In this perspective, a European foreign policy is likely to be more regional than global.[18] Its concerns will be primarily directed to the Mediterranean, the Middle East, and Africa. It may play a larger economic role abroad, but politically it is likely to be focused on the North-South axis where its national interests are most vulnerable and its limited power most effective. Yet the Common Market's many economic arrangements with non-members have given Europe political leverage that goes well beyond the confines of its geographical region. The sight of non-Europeans from as far away as Australia and New Zealand queuing up, cap in hand, for favors from the Community has a certain political effect on the Europeans' consciousness of what uniting can do for them. Moreover, these preferential arrangements and their presumed impact on United States trade with the countries that get them will remain a sore point between America and the new Europe.

China is, in the meantime, likely to see Europe as most valuable as a counterweight to Soviet influence in Europe. The long-term aim of Chinese policy—to support dissident states in Eastern Europe such as Yugoslavia and Rumania —certainly assumes a strong Europe as yet another constraint upon the power of imperialistic Russia. For this reason, China does not welcome a European Security Conference or mutual and balanced force reductions that could allow Russia even more freedom to concentrate on her eastern border. Peking is developing a European policy that would encourage a strong European Community which could challenge Russia, or at least be strong enough to pose a potential threat to Soviet hegemony in the event of American withdrawal.

The need for a European defense grouping becomes the inevitable corollary of an independent Europe, if it is to be capable of playing even a regional role in the global balance of power. A kind of European Defense Community, as part of or connected to the Atlantic Alliance, is likely to be one quite different from the EDC formulations of the 1950s with their emphasis on integration. In this sense, as in others, a more Gaullist Europe is likely to emerge.[19]

Beyond a European defense grouping lurks the problem that has bedeviled relations between Europe and America for over twenty years—the question of Europe's nuclear capability and America's nuclear guarantee. Without rehashing the old argument that de Gaulle raised when Russia had achieved rough nuclear parity with America, i.e., will the United States risk nuclear destruction for Paris, the subject of the credibility of the American nuclear guarantees simply will not go away. From Europe's perspective, the SALT agreement is hardly likely to strengthen the United States commitment. American domestic pressures—clearly perceived by the Europeans—for military withdrawal and for protectionism in trade undermine our commitments no matter how often an American President reiterates them. Finally, there is the probability—and desideratum—of a European nuclear force.

Logic compels its eventual emergence, no matter what the United States attitude toward such a force may be. Harold Wilson, *before* he became Labour's Prime Minister, suggested that Britain should dump its nuclear force into the sea, for all the good it did and all the money it cost. As Prime Minister he did not do what he said. France, determined in 1954 to build her own nuclear force, rebuffed in her soundings for a United States–United Kingdom–France Triumvirate in 1958, willing to defy world opinion by conducting nuclear tests in the atmosphere, excluded from American nuclear technology by the United States Congress, has no intentions of abandoning her *force de frappe*. However, the French and British forces are essentially complementary. An *entente nucléaire*, though not in the offing, has been hinted at by Prime Minister Edward Heath. To some degree, the fate of a European force still lies with the United States government. Washington could, if it chose to interpret the MacMahon Act differently, offer the French nuclear aid. In any case, by the late 1970s the restraints put on the transfer of nuclear technology from Britain to France (because of Britain's special arrangements to obtain nuclear assistance from Washington) will expire. If Washington chose to, it could assist in the Europeanization of a nuclear force, leaving it to the Europeans themselves to work out satisfactory arrangements with West Germany and the other members of the Community.

In any case, for Washington to expend all its efforts to discourage a European nuclear force—and the inevitable concomitants of independence that such a force would imply—would be both fruitless and probably self-defeating. Better to help than to hinder your ally in order to keep him your ally. Détente in Europe, arms-control agreements in Central Europe, a stronger economic as well as political community, seem indeed to be the directions in which Europe is heading. For many years Washington has proclaimed its commitment to European unity. The Europe it may get may be an unmanageable creature, but its evolution seems inevitable. If a balance of power—particularly a five-power one—has any chance of becoming meaningful, it would be better that it come about with American assistance. Allies, not a series of client-states, is the true meaning of a viable balance of great powers.

EIGHT

The nuclear question always looms large when consideration of the changing American–Japanese relationship is analyzed. Of America's major allies Japan has probably undergone the most traumatic shocks in the changed environment that occurred in the 1970s. The unheralded American approach to Peking, followed hard upon by a Russian démarche to Tokyo by the Foreign Minister Andrei Gromyko, the August 1971, United States economic policies were aimed more explicitly at Japan than at any other power—these events made Japan acutely aware of her great national economic power while dramatizing her strategic and political vulnerability. In explicating America's New Economic Policy, President Nixon underscored Japan's trade advantages as providing the thrust of America's own economic nationalism:

We found ourselves confronted with intense and increasing competition from other major industrialized nations. As one measure of this between 1960 and 1971 Japan's exports increased by 242 percent. . . . It means that the old days, in which we were willing to accept arrangements which put us at a competitive disadvantage with respect to our trading partners, are gone–and the old policies must go with them. . . . Our total reserves dwindled from $21 billion in 1946 to roughly $12 billion at the end of 1971, and, while all this was happening, many of our major trading partners still maintained distorted exchange rates–which favored their exports and hampered ours–and trade barriers which had the effect of limiting the access of United States products to their markets.[20]

If such talk were simply confined to monetary matters, however, the Japanese would eventually find themselves only forced to upvalue the yen; but economic pressures are far from the only new realities which the Japanese must adjust to. A more profound adjustment affects Japan's role in the Far East and how—if at all—she should play any part in establishing a four-power balance of power in Asia which the United States may desire and the Chinese may fear.

"The more you [Americans] talk about balance of power, the more it means to us that we have the power"—this was the reaction of one thoughtful Japanese.[21] Such a concept inevitably leads to considerations of Japan as a nuclear power. Such a role is not an easy one for the Japanese to contemplate. Though Gaullism may be her fate, the progression from dependence (on the United States) to Gaullism, and possibly neutralism, is not an easy path. Japan's pride in her economic gigantism has not yet been translated into the pride of the poker-playing great power that many seem to expect of her. Charges, however, by American officials that Japan is enjoying a "free ride" on defense (currently about 1 percent of her gross national product as compared with America's 8 percent), which in turn gives her a competitive trade advantage, can as easily stimulate Japan to turn her energies to nuclear weapons as to increasing her largely unusable conventional forces. Such troops, moreover, would not even have the weight of being a viable military deterrent, as the French concluded in the 1950s.

But what if Japan decided to play a greater part in the regional balance of power in East Asia and the Pacific? Though it would be very convenient from an American viewpoint for Japan to increase her economic aid to poorer countries in Southeast Asia while maintaining ever-stronger conventional defense forces, there is a serious flaw in the proposition that this is a role Japan will be content to assume, i.e., changing the nature of her alliance with the United States to one of equality. Professor Edwin Reischauer, former United States Ambassador to Japan, has expressed just such doubts over Tokyo's ability to make such a transition. He has said that Japan may not be able to make this change "from a sense of dependence on the United States (and some fear of being inferior) to an ability to accept the United States as an interdependent equal." The result could be a loosening of ties between Japan and the United States, even an American withdrawal from playing a significant role in East Asia and Japan's going nuclear.[22]

According to Zbigniew Brzezinski, by 1975 Japan will be in a "proto-nuclear posture." With increasing United States withdrawals of forces in the area, Japan could be further tempted to pick up the nuclear option. Brzezinski then recommends that though this may not be a desirable course, from Washington's viewpoint, if Japan does go nuclear the United States should assist it at this point of decision.[23] This would certainly help Washington to avoid the errors it made in regard to France's nuclear program, i.e., trying to stop the inevitable. Moreover, United States assistance could be a guard against Gaullism, and even prove to be a strengthening factor in the alliance. For to demand of a major ally to accept somewhat the status of a client-state—no matter what the magnitude—is perhaps to ask the impossible and thus to reap a resurgence of Japanese militarism and nationalism that would undermine rather than contribute to the regional balance of power that seems to be forming in the wake of United States withdrawal from the Asian mainland. In sum, if viewed solely in the context of

American–Japanese relations, a Japanese nuclear force is something that Washington might choose to assist. But in the global context a nuclear Japan, aided by the United States, would certainly damage the dual rapprochements that Washington seeks with Moscow and Peking, even though the two Communist powers might be forced to live with a nuclear Japan just as Russia had to come to terms with a rearmed West Germany.

The quadrilateral balance of power that may develop in Asia would be an evolution arising out of several developments: continued Sino–Soviet hostility, the decline of American power in Asia combined with Washington's desire to maintain its alliance with Japan while expanding its new opening to China. By trying to prevent any one power from becoming preponderant the quadrilateral rationale evolves. Only if America chooses to become a mid-Pacific rather than a Western Pacific power is such a situation unlikely to occur. But the United States may find withdrawal to the mid-Pacific as dangerous as its intervention in Southeast Asia. Fearful of Japan, China *and* Russia may come to prefer the Japanese connection with a relatively distant United States to the threat of uninhibited Japanese nationalism.

The four-power balance of power in East Asia, then, is likely to be a dynamic rather than a static one. Chinese and Russian fears of Japanese militarism, American fear of Japanese economic strength, Russia's desire to leap-frog China by forming a closer tie with Japan, Japan's desire to allay Chinese fears as well as to penetrate the Chinese market— such an interplay among great powers is elastic but need not be dangerous to world peace. There can be the most careful attention to sensibility. But no nation is likely to establish an hegemony in the region; fluidity is not going to be confined merely to the economic level. Politics—and its military-strategic concomitants—will be decisive factors. Having cut China into the deal, neither Japan nor Russia nor America is likely to feel secure enough to quit the game.

NINE

As Algeria was for General de Gaulle, the ultimate resolution of the Indochina War is the final condition for success in the remaking of American foreign policy. Throughout all the long years of American intervention—from the 16,000 advisers sent by President Kennedy to the half million American troops who were fighting in Vietnam when Nixon was elected—the ability of a small power like North Vietnam to manipulate the big powers points up the problem of working within an undefined balance of power. In a sense all three great powers were hostages to Hanoi. Such a condition was inevitable so long as the three great powers were unable to act in concert to impose their collective will.

But even between North Vietnam's two allies, a collective will was usually absent. Because of the Sino–Soviet split, Russia and China, rather than acting together, had to bid against one another for favor with Hanoi. Even if the two Communist powers had wanted to aid Washington in gaining a settlement, neither power could exact decisive influence over North Vietnam. Indeed, since the Laos settlement in 1962, it was evident that neither Moscow nor Peking controlled Hanoi, while Hanoi could insist that both Communist giants furnish help, even if they did so somewhat reluctantly.[24]

Then, when the Nixon administration moved ahead to establish closer contacts with Peking and conclude far-reaching agreements with Moscow, neither Russia nor China wanted to endanger its improved relations with the United States. Thus, since neither Moscow nor Peking could dictate policy to Hanoi in order to assist Washington in finding a way out—even if they had wanted to—Washington was finally forced to deal with Hanoi alone. Despite numerous discussions on how to end the Indochina War with leaders in Peking and Moscow, Henry Kissinger pointed out, even prior to the Peking and Moscow summits, that America expected "to settle this war with Hanoi, not with Moscow and not with Peking." [25]

This is not to say that Moscow and Peking never made their position clear to Hanoi. Russia, in fact, did so on half a dozen or more occasions during the first stages of the Paris negotiations in 1968–1969. In a secret National Security Council study, made at the request of the President on January 21, 1969, it was revealed that the Russians either suggested or modified the formula ultimately accepted by both sides. The analysis from the State Department declared that the Soviet Ambassador "intervened constructively, acting under both general guidelines and explicit instructions from Moscow." However, it was "not clear whether it was necessary for [the Russians] to bring pressure on the North Vietnamese to bring about a compromise." Further, it was quite possible that the North Vietnamese "employed the Soviets as intermediaries to convey positions upon which they had already decided themselves, so that they would not have to 'lose face' by making concessions directly to us." While the State Department analysts believed that whenever the Soviets "consider it warranted," they could "continue to stake out tough Hanoi bargaining positions, explore United States thinking . . . and utilize their leverage upon Hanoi in measured, highly selective and carefully timed fashion," the American military commentators held a different view. Their analysts reported that "as far as our knowledge of how Hanoi thinks and feels, we see through the glass darkly if at all." But on the basis of intelligence derived from Hanoi's diplomatic connections in Moscow and Peking, "there does not appear to be significant pressure by Moscow or Peking on North Vietnam."

Even after that period the administration undoubtedly tried to use Moscow as a conduit for making United States positions on the war known to Hanoi. Moreover, the Nixon administration also had good connections in Peking that had not been previously available. As time wore on, the Chinese voiced less and less opposition to a negotiated settlement, probably because they came more and more to believe that the Americans were going to get out of Indochina "come what may" (as Nixon put it to de Gaulle) and wanted to reduce Soviet influence in the region.

But to assume that the Chinese would have tried to pressure Hanoi into accepting American terms to end the war would probably be misleading. Chou En-lai declared openly that the Vietnamese would resist any such pressures. He said to a group of American visitors in June 1972, that feudal China had tried to subdue them and failed, as had France. He also stressed the fact that he felt he had been betrayed by signing the Geneva Accords of 1954, which partitioned the country and then promised free elections within two years. "I have said this to Premier Pham Van Dong [of North Vietnam]," Chou En-lai explained. "We committed a mistake in signing the Geneva agreements, and I was the representative who put his signature to that agreement." [26]

American perceptions in regard to the independence of the North Vietnamese leadership also changed. By shedding the notion that the Indochina War was part of the "deepening shadow" of China, as Lyndon Johnson put it, Washington concluded that a little friendly leverage from Moscow or Peking would not change Hanoi from pursuing its own chosen course, though such leverage would certainly be useful if not decisive.

For the small power, manipulation of the great powers is possible only when there is conflict among the great. This was true when the United States and the Soviet Union fought for ideological allies in Africa in the 1950s and early 1960s, when nonalignment implied to the Americans that such "neutralism" was not to choose our side in the cold war. Balance-of-power politics, unless the great powers are prepared to act in concert to impose their will, give great scope for maneuverability to the small.

Nixon believed after his Moscow summit meeting that "it is precisely the fact that the elements of balance now exist that gives us a rare opportunity to create a system of stability that can maintain the peace not just for a generation— but we hope beyond." [27]

But we live in a world of competing nationalisms whether we like it or not. Not only is neo-nationalism on the rise among the nations of the third world but it has characterized the policies of the United States, China, Russia, Japan, and, to some degree, Europe. Yet these are the same five powers which Nixon saw as being able to "create a system of stability." The interplay of the great powers in pursuing balance-of-power politics is thus likely to be a dangerous game. Since we live in a world of competing nationalisms, the question is not can we live with them but how?

NOTES

1. See Earl C. Ravenal's article, "The Nixon Doctrine and Our Asian Commitments," *Foreign Affairs*, January 1971, p. 201.

2. Richard Nixon, *U.S. Foreign Policy for the 1970's. A New Strategy for Peace*. Washington, D.C.: U.S. Government Printing Office, February 18, 1970, pp. 128–129.

3. See the discussion of the concept of "access and influence" by Marshall Shulman, "What Does Security Mean Today?" *Foreign Affairs*, July 1971.

4. See Ronald Steel, "A Spheres of Influence Policy," in *Foreign Policy*, Nos. 5 and 6, 1971–1972, pp. 111 and 150.

5. From an essay by Earl C. Ravenal, "Beyond the Balance of Power," to be included in a forthcoming book by the same author.

6. John C. Campbell and Helen Caruso, *The West and the Middle East*. New York: Council Papers on International Affairs, No. 1, 1972, p. 8.

7. See Richard Nixon, *U.S. Foreign Policy for the 1970's: Building for Peace*. Washington, D.C.: U.S. Government Printing Office, February 25, 1971.

8. See William J. Barnds, "India-Pakistan and American Realpolitik," *Christianity and Crisis*, June 25, 1972, p. 148.

9. *The New York Times*, January 16, 1972.

10. Ross Terrill, *The 800,000,000*. Boston: Atlantic-Little, Brown, 1972, p. 145.

11. Henry Kissinger, "Domestic Structure and Foreign Policy" *Daedalus*, Spring 1966, p. 521.

12. Richard Nixon, "The Real Road to Peace," *U.S. News and World Report*, June 26, 1972, p. 33.

13. See Earl C. Ravenal, "China Statement: Between the Lines," *The Washington Post*, March 5, 1972.
14. *The New York Times*, June 1, 1972.
15. See Marshall D. Shulman, "Political Problems for Both Sides," *The Washington Post*, June 4, 1972.
16. *The New York Times*, June 1, 1972.
17. Quoted by I.F. Stone in his article, "The New Shape of Nixon's World," *The New York Review of Books*, June 29, 1972, p. 12.
18. See Andrew Pierre, "Europe and America in a Pentagonal World," *Survey*, No. 1 (82), Winter 1972, pp. 187 ff.
19. See Francois Duchene, "A New European Defense Community," *Foreign Affairs*, October 1971.
20. Nixon, "The Real Road to Peace," p. 38.
21. William P. Bundy, "The View from Japan," *Newsweek*, May 1, 1972, p. 46.
22. See Reischauer quotation in "A New Sort of Japan," *The Economist*, June 17–23, 1972, p. 18.
23. See Zbigniew Brzezinski, *The Fragile Blossom*. New York: Harper and Row, 1972.
24. William P. Bundy, "Doubtful Premises," *Newsweek*, May 22, 1972, p. 50.
25. *The New York Times*, January 27, 1972.
26. *The New York Times*, June 17, 1972.
27. Nixon, "The Real Road to Peace," p. 40.

III

ON NAVIGATION

The essential fallacy of Castlereagh's political philosophy was that by exaggerating the general need for "repose" he sought to enforce static principles upon a dynamic world.

—Sir Harold Nicolson

The Pilot, vanquish'd by the Pow'r Divine,
Soon clos'd his swimming Eyes, and lay supine.
Scarce were his Limbs extended at their length,
The God, insulting with superior Strength,
Fell heavy on him, plung'd him in the Sea,
And, with the Stern, the Rudder tore away.
Headlong he fell, and struggling in the Main,
Cry'd out for helping hands, but cry'd in vain:
The Victor Demon mounts obscure in Air;
While the Ship sails without the Pilot's care.

—Dryden's Aeneid

ONE

It has become fashionable in our attempts to discover what went wrong with America's postwar global engagement to concentrate on the decision-making process. But studies on how decisions are made, as Dean Acheson allegedly said, tend to read like a Machiavelli for weak princes. What one learns from discussions on the decision-making process is often misleading because of the concentration on process and proceeding rather than on substantive rationale. They ask *how* decisions were made when they should be asking why. The best organized machinery in assisting in the decision-making process is less important than the perceptions that affect those who formulate our foreign policy at the highest level. For example, in the studies of the Nassau agreements of 1962 which gave to the British the submarine-launched Polaris missile after the United States refused further funding for development of the air-to-ground Skybolt missiles, the crucial decision was made by President Kennedy. But he acted as he did essentially in order to help the British Prime Minister Harold Macmillan out of an embarrassing political situation which might have cost the Tories dearly at election time. Though the crisis was escalated to the top level by a series of bureaucratic miscalculations, Kennedy's decision was made outside the realm of bureaucratic politics.[1]

There were a number of choices available to Kennedy including inviting General de Gaulle to Nassau if necessary. It was not so much the machinery that was at fault in the

ill-chosen decision to prolong the "special relationship" between America and Britain but rather the perceptions of
the President himself. How he saw Macmillan and how he
behaved toward him—this was the essence of decision and
derived precisely from his perceptions of the situation. It
may also be that Macmillan was not wholly honest with
Kennedy over his recent conversations with de Gaulle at
Rambouillet on prospects for British entry into the Common Market. Finally, and in my view most likely, after
President Eisenhower rebuffed de Gaulle's proposed directorate of the United States–United Kingdom–France in
1958, de Gaulle was determined to go his own way. The
Nassau episode, by this reading, gave the General the ex-
cuse for vetoing British entry into Europe he was looking for
anyway.

The interplay of the perceptions of these three men (one
of whom, de Gaulle, rarely if ever confided in his subordi-
nates) were, however, crucial in a turning point in United
States foreign policy—the beginning of the end of the
"grand design" for American–European relations.

So, too, as we have seen earlier, it was the perceptions of
the architects of postwar American foreign policy that
shaped its design; the implementation of this policy was
sometimes ill and sometimes well carried out but the overall
thrust would not have greatly changed once certain perceptions were deeply held. We have seen how the formulations
embodied in Kennan's "X" article reinforced the feeling
that was growing among United States policymakers that
Russia was to become our adversary rather than our ally. If
there was any point at which these perceptions became
fixed, it probably came, as Arthur Krock and others have
pointed out, even earlier, after a speech given by Stalin in

February 1946. This was, in Krock's words, "a declaration of total and unending world war to destroy the capitalist system." [2] Dean Acheson stated (March 20, 1970) categorically that "George Kennan's containment article was a description of what was happening anyway." What resulted from these perceptions was America's conduct in the quarter century of the cold war that followed. By and large, this was a clear policy, one that could be presented without ambiguity.

By what was wrongly perceived to be what Charles Gati has called "a relatively simple explanation of the Soviet challenge in world affairs as well as an equally simple prescription for American foreign policy to meet that challenge," [3] Kennan's article became distorted and was so presented to the public. Though Kennan's views were, in fact, more complex than when they were presented by others, they could be and were seen by the American people in terms which fitted in with the rather Manichean strain that runs through the American tradition, the struggle between good and evil, between darkness and light. One needs but to read Cooper, Hawthorne, and Melville to see how deeply ingrained are these feelings.

As the cold war has drawn to a close, however, as perceptions of the role America should play in the world have been questioned, there are those who yearn for a policy as apparently clear-cut as were the policies formulated in the late 1940s. Such men often welcome change but are disturbed by the lack of clear solutions. It seems to me that only rarely is there a period in history when foreign policy can be defined as unambiguously as United States foreign policy was spelled out twenty-five years ago. Today, there is a new foreign policy in the making, but it is being made in a world far more chaotic than the immediate postwar world. There are more chessboards and more players; there are transnational forces that operate both against and alongside neo-nationalistic trends. Nothing is more dangerous than to allow wishful thinking to permeate policy; what we would like we cannot will into being.

There has always been a dialectic between idealism and realism in a wise foreign policy, and no one has made that clearer than Lord Palmerston a century ago. The famous dictum Palmerston laid down was: "We have no eternal allies and we have no perpetual enemies. Our interests are eternal and perpetual, and those interests it is our duty to follow." Here, then, is the so-called realist position. But, in the same speech, Palmerston went on to explain that the policy of England was also "to be the champion of justice and right: pursuing that course with moderation and prudence, not becoming the Quixote of the world, but giving her moral sanction and support wherever she thinks justice is, and whenever she thinks that wrong has been done."

If these cautionary words can serve as a general statement of the aims of a nation that would pursue a wise foreign policy, then we can hazard a set of perceptions of how the world looks from the perspective of the 1970s. Such perceptions must be put forth with caution, and may be distorted. But in the setting of a new foreign policy, one must risk one's own apprehension of what might be.

A controlling metaphor might be that of the navigator. He must be a skillful pilot who knows the tides and currents; he must understand that there are times when it is foolhardy to buck such elements. He must also take note of shoals, that "shelfy Coast," in Dryden's Virgil, "long infamous for ships and sailors lost; and white with Bones." How to avoid that "shelfy Coast" while contending with wind and tide and current that may be driving you toward just such a reef—this is the dilemma for the navigator. Finally, there is the character of the navigator himself: how responsible is he? Will he, like Aeneas' navigator Palinurus, fall asleep, "and struggling in the Main, Cry'd out for helping hands, but cry'd in vain." In the *Aeneid* it was not enough for Palinurus to have led the fleet safely between Scylla and Charybdis; he must never falter; failing once he lost all. There are ways by which a skilled pilot can erect a make-shift jury rig if his mast breaks; it may indeed be all that he can do to work with the elements that buffet him and still avoid the "shelfy Coast." Like the wise statesman, the navigator must deal with what is and what may lie ahead.[4]

TWO

As I have indicated, two schools of thought have contended for an approach to the international system. And, as we have also seen, it is the statist rather than the federalist approach which is in the ascendancy in the post-postwar world. For much of the postwar era, however, the so-called federalist approach was advocated by American policymak-ers, particularly those in the State Department. Whether it be the grand design of a United States of Europe or those regional groupings which Walt Rostow, President Johnson's Special Assistant for National Security, espoused, the United States seemed to feel that its own federalist system should be—and at times could be—the model for stability. As Harry McPherson described it in his invaluable memoir, *A Political Education*:

Rostow believed that poor nations in Asia, Africa, and Latin America were beginning to pool their resources and to commit themselves to the common defense of their regions. . . . It seemed plausible and therefore hopeful. But it was based on several shaky premises: that the frail regional organizations based in Bangkok or Addis Ababa represented something more than ideas, and could actually commit the governments of their regions to common actions; that the primordial animosities of race and religion, and the new demands of national pride, would yield to unproved theories of economic and political cooperation.[5]

The matrix for the model derived from America's own success in federalism, although it has been misapplied when it was hoped that it could be extended to other parts of the globe. Reading the Federalist Papers of Hamilton, Jay, and Madison reveals how difficult was the struggle to make a federal republic of a confederation of states. Even those Hamiltonians who believed that certain objective forces could make a nation saw things less clearly than did Washington himself. The facts were that if each state's special interests were considered, there would have been no whole. The thirteen original colonies, however, had already attained an inchoate reality by the end of the Revolution: language, customs, and shared values born out of the experience of revolution. John Jay, in 1787, arguing for a federal constitution, spoke eloquently for the community of America. "Providence," he wrote, "has been pleased to give this one connected country to one united people—a people descended from the same ancestors, speaking the same language, professing the same religion, attached to the same principles of government, very similar in their manners and customs, and who, by their joint counsels, arms, and efforts, fighting side by side throughout a long and bloody war, have nobly established their general liberty and independence."

There was, as Jay saw, a reality to build on. The truncated Europe that emerged after 1946 to form an entity was also a group of nations not formed so much by abstract, objective forces as by the communality that had already existed. De Gasperi, Adenauer, Schuman—these three men saw in Europe's heritage a Roman Europe with its legal traditions, its culture, its religion. This was the remembered unity of Europe. Upon such foundation the various economic and technocratic bureaucracies were erected. When those outside Europe have projected a Wilsonian view upon the ancient continent, they have often failed to perceive the underlying unity. The Multilateral Nuclear Force, the European Defense Community—these schemes failed because they were grounded in a false perception of political reality. The nationalistic tendencies which gave impetus to the Roman Europe concept of the postwar world were either conveniently ignored or wished away by the American desire to see a unified Europe that would be both benevolent and non-nationalistic.

The United States, however, never really abandoned its own nationalistic stance, particularly in the matter of defense. And in the last decade Europe has been treated less as an ally than as a client-state. True, there has been as yet no "Europe" to deal with. The pentagonal world is still very much in the making. But it is dangerous to argue that since there are in truth only two "great powers," the other three, since they are not of the same magnitude, will not act as great power centers and be treated as such.

The perception of whether or not a nation is a great power lies not only in the actions of that power but in the eye of the beholder. The fact that China's gross national product only rivals Italy's does not make Italy a great power. Nor does India's vast population as yet make her a great power. Yet China can strut upon the world's stage as a great power, armed with her ideology, her economic potential, and her population; and she will be treated as such.

The reality then is resurgent nationalism, and any balance-of-power concept must first take this into consideration. Only by dealing first with the great power configurations that either now exist or are potential can one go on to deal with other transnational forces that appear to transcend the nation-state but, in fact, cannot often act independently of it. To talk about "our endangered planet," as though by signalling the dangers of overpopulation, multinational corporations, wastage both moral and physical of man's resources, without considering the viability—indeed the vitality—of the nation-state is to exhort rather than to act, to spy out the "shelfy Coast" and yet be unable to avoid it because one is unwilling to deal with the forces at hand. You cannot go beyond the balance of power by disregarding it.

THREE

Can there be an international system then that rejects a world of five power centers for a world of non-Communist, advanced industrial nations?* Is such a configuration a way

* By advanced industrial nations I mean essentially the Group of Ten of the International Monetary Fund comprising Belgium, Canada, France, West Germany, Italy, Japan, the Netherlands, Sweden, the United Kingdom, and the United States.

of transcending a global balance of power and thus allowing us to deal effectively with those transnational forces that both threaten and favor us? The greatest problem posed by the concept of a community of advanced industrial nations is its relation to the rest of the world. Not only is there the tension that could result from the division between the rich and poor but also the temptation toward exclusion of the Communist nations which could undermine the policies of détente, entente, and cooperation that the non-Communist world now seeks.

Despite the hopes voiced by those who would see in such a community a pooled effort of aid to the poorer countries and a concerted opening to the Communist world, such concepts, while theoretically attractive, are hard to envisage as an entity for cooperation much beyond the international monetary field where a communality of interests already exists.

The most difficult obstacle to overcome is the question of security. While the United States can extend its nuclear wings over both Europe and Japan if it chooses, it is well-nigh impossible to envisage Japanese security interests dovetailing with Europe's. Either both power centers will remain allied closely to America or they will go their own separate ways. This is a far cry from a concerted policy.

Alastair Buchan has further pointed out that in an age when military power may play a less dominating role, the American–Japanese–European triangle is of far less importance. In a system based on "multiple coexistence," there is great value in preserving autonomy. "The autonomous state or civilization," Buchan maintains, "has a great deal of vitality and we are more likely to live in relative tranquility if we respect this differentiation while opposing the temptations of universality for our own values or the claims of other politics." [6]

North–South relations may develop, as they already have, between separate power centers of the advanced industrial societies and the third world. The United States, however, might well choose a policy of decoupling unilaterally from aid and investment in much of the third world. We could even decide, as Richard Cooper and Joseph Nye have pointed out, to give "no bilateral financial assistance except for disaster relief and other immediate but limited humanitarian purposes." [7] Investment is more important for the third world than for the United States. American aid could be funnelled through multilateral, international agencies such as the International Monetary Fund and the World Bank. Transnational social and cultural concerns are another matter; but in the case of the United States, they may apply to Israel and Africa more appropriately than to South America which has often been thought of as the traditional third world area of American interest.

In Africa, on the other hand, a close economic relationship exists with Europe; in South America, Japan is already challenging the United States for economic penetration and influence. Miriam Camps has wisely pointed out that it seems reasonably clear that this group of advanced countries is "not yet ready—intellectually, psychologically, bureaucratically—for the radical course of much more integration of our economies, much more coordination of policy, and much more collective management." [8]

If, then, such a community of advanced industrial societies is unlikely to emerge in the foreseeable future, then indeed we are left with the strategic balance of power among the five as a precondition for dealing with transnational forces.

FOUR

In coping with the balance of power and with those transnational forces that may lead America into a variety of involvements she has never anticipated, the first question to be confronted is the rise of neo-nationalism and America's reaction to it. I have said earlier that, like it or not, we now live in a world of contending nationalisms. America's behavior over the past few years has undoubtedly contributed to this nationalism. A new American foreign policy cannot wish away the emerging balance of power (that it has in part helped create), but it can preserve its major alliances and mitigate its own neo-nationalistic tendencies as it participates in the formation of a new international order. America need be neither isolationist nor isolated. And it is the latter position that she is most likely to find herself in if proper care is not paid to the course she lays out.

One of the most striking phenomena that has occurred in the waning years of the cold war has been the erosion of our relations with our major allies. This could easily reach the point of an American attempt—though not necessarily a conscious one—at reduction of allies to the position of client-states. It could imply a mercenary relationship; yet, in the case of major allies, it is in the interest of the United States that they maintain and increase their strength and independence.

One can measure the degree of consultation that has diminished by recalling the need felt by Washington to have British approbation during the Korean War, or the advice

of Anthony Eden in 1954 during United States delibera-
tions over whether or not to aid the French with direct
military assistance during the siege of Dien Bien Phu. Since
Suez—when the divergence of American and European interests was clearest—there has been an increasing tendency for the United States to go it alone. The rejection of
de Gaulle's proposed directorate in 1958 was one more step
in alienating American policy from that of one of her major
allies. The decision not to assist the French nuclear force,
even when it was inevitable that the *force de frappe* would
be built, alienated United States policy still further from
France's. At the same time, the refusal of the British to join
the burgeoning institutions of the Common Market, such as
the European Defense Community and the Coal and Steel
Community in the 1950s, rendered Europe a less viable entity to deal with. And de Gaulle's arrival on the scene in
1958 further complicated—if not to say exacerbated—the
situation. Unwilling to surrender our own control over strategic weapons or, indeed, give up one jot of sovereignty, we
urged the Europeans to do precisely the opposite of what we
ourselves were prepared to do. The configuration of American and European policies made a series of client-state relationships more rather than less likely to emerge as the pattern of American–European relations.

Under the Nixon-Kissinger regimen the tendency to let
Europe go its own way became more pronounced. Indeed,
under President Johnson, United States policy toward Europe—no doubt largely because of preoccupation with
Southeast Asia—became one of benign neglect. As Washington no longer fostered American plans on the Europeans,
the Common Market countries began to engender a unity
that went beyond agreements on the price of beet sugar.

The enlarged Europe of the Ten is coordinating policy, albeit by fits and starts. Though "Europe" may not exist as a great power in the strict sense of the word, a European consensus is growing, and as it does so, Washington will have to face up to new policies to cope with the changed postwar world it did so much to create.

As we have seen, there will certainly be questions of defense to contend with. Logic compels one to believe that the French and the British will—eventually—have to abandon their *separate* nuclear forces. But this does not mean discarding them. Can the United States play a useful role in assisting a truly European nuclear grouping? The likelihood that such a group will emerge anyway makes this hardly a moot question. A European nuclear role within the Atlantic Alliance could be an important aim of United States foreign policy. Moreover, France's emergence as a nuclear power has not encouraged West Germany to follow the same path. Nonproliferation as it was seen ten years ago is no longer as relevant to Europe as it is to the rest of the world. In any case, when the present agreement with Great Britain—allowing United States assistance to Britain while denying it to France—expires in 1974, America will be forced to reexamine her policies.

A new nuclear-sharing policy with France, as Andrew Pierre has pointed out, "would not require a change in the United States atomic energy legislation since France would now qualify under the 1958 amendments permitting assistance to those states which have already demonstrated 'substantial progress' in a nuclear-weapons program of their own. But it would have to receive the support of the Joint Committee on Atomic Energy and of the Congress as a whole. This might be more readily obtained if it were done in conjunction with an understanding that there was to be a limited reduction of United States forces in Europe." [9]

There is a feeling in Europe and in America, particularly under pressure from the Senate, that there *will* be American troop reductions in Europe. These may be accomplished in conjunction with mutual and balanced force reductions in agreement with the Soviet Union; they may be accomplished as part of a European Security Conference. However it is done, force reductions are inevitable: the determination of their level is the key problem. But this, too, will force Europe to re-evaluate her own defense posture. She may choose a new, looser form of a European Defense Community of a non-nuclear character but without the integration proposed in the early 1950s. She may combine some form of a defense community with a European Nuclear Committee which could have Britain and France as the nucleus of the program but include representation by non-nuclear countries.

These projections will serve to make Europe both more independent of the United States and a more reliable ally. It will remove the client-state stigma, a stigma which has already become obsolete in the monetary field.

But just as the United States must avoid the uncouth and often counterproductive tactics employed by the then Secretary of the Treasury John Connally in his monetary dealings with the Europeans in the summer of 1971, so, too, a thought-out strategy involving our military commitments must be made without the singularly ill-considered shocks delivered unilaterally by Washington. These caused our major allies to respond with fear and repugnance to what seemed like America's own embrace of neo-nationalism and to undermine the essential fundaments of an alliance. There is no inherent reason why the European alliance cannot be preserved within a global balance of power that includes China, Russia, and Japan.

Similarly, with regard to Japan, the Nixon shocks of 1971—unilateral imposition of the 10 percent surcharge on imports, re-establishment of relations with Peking, support for China's entry into the United Nations—served to remind Japan of her own political and military vulnerability. While the United States seems to be aiming at a quadrilateral balance of power in East Asia, one that would involve Japan, China, Russia, and the United States, Washington also wants to preserve its alliance with Tokyo. Such aims are not incompatible. But to do so not only means a more delicate handling of Japanese sensibilities, so that an American reversal of policy toward China should not undermine, as it did, previous United States efforts to align Japanese policy with American policy toward Peking; it also involves the nuclear question. For if Japan decides to go nuclear, nothing would be more counterproductive than to pursue a policy toward Japan that paralleled our attitude toward France. This is not to imply that the United States should encourage Japan in nuclear armament; indeed, such a change of Japanese military posture would stir up the fires of resentment that still burn throughout the former Greater East Asia Co-Prosperity Sphere. But the American–Japanese alliance serves as a protection not only against the hegemony in East Asia of Japan but also against that of the Soviet Union and China.

As noted before, Japan's going nuclear is the last thing that Russia or China would like to see happen. And it is in part for this reason that an American presence in the Far East is no longer regarded by Moscow and Peking as the menace it once seemed. To begin with, there seems little question that United States forces in mainland Asia and Japan (as in Europe) will be reduced. Japan, nuclear or not, is a power not lightly regarded by Russia and China. Though Chinese sources have disavowed Chou En-lai's alleged statements to American congressional leaders that China desired a continued American "presence" in the Far East,[10] in fact a reduced but significant United States presence, one that would not threaten China but contain Japan and free China to defend herself against the Soviet Union, would be very much to China's (as well as to Korea's) interest.

If the *sine qua non* of such a presence is American withdrawal from Indochina, then one could hazard the guess that Peking accepts ultimate United States disengagement from Southeast Asia while anticipating continued American involvement in the Far East. By encouraging a four-power balance of power in East Asia, the United States will have to reap the seeds it has sown. A more nationalistic and, perhaps eventually, a nuclear Japan may be the fruit of this policy. Already there are signs that both Moscow and Peking desire ever closer relations with Japan. Tokyo is not likely, after the dramatic changes in American policy since 1968, to rebuff such overtures.

FIVE

And so, in a world of competing nationalisms, America is faced, on the one hand, with more independent if not to say more truculent allies, and on the other hand, with her de-

sire not to loosen her ties with her allies to such an extent
that they are ripped asunder. Even those critics who envisage a five-power world in which Japan and Europe act as
independent powers must face up to the fact that it will be
some time to come before either power center can act independently as an economic, military, and political force. For
this same reason it is paradoxically less important whether
or not they constitute "full-fledged" powers in the Metternichian sense than centers of power with enough weight to
make them major factors in the international system. No alliance is permanent and there is nothing immutable in either the United States–Japan or United States–Europe alliance. Ripeness, as both Shakespeare and de Gaulle
recognized, is all. And, at least in the next decade, the end
of an alliance with either Japan or Europe has hardly
reached that point where either power center would be
ready or willing to accept the status as an orphan.

We must now look to that "shelfy Coast" which is indif-
ferent to the strategic current that impels nations forward.
The balance of power has been traditionally an attempt to
achieve equilibrium; though it has always been a schema
aimed at containing the overweening ambitions of any one
great power, it is no longer being used to contain Communist territorial expansion. To describe the new balance of
power as a disguised form of containment (as it was practiced under Truman in specific geographic areas and later
globalized under Eisenhower) is a misreading of the
changed global environment. Without some form of equilibrium it would be well-nigh impossible to cooperate with
other major powers on projects which involve transnational
forces. But such an equilibrium or balance of power must

not be static but based on the concept, already mentioned, of allowing to the great powers global access and influence rather than territorial trade-offs and spheres of influence. The equilibrium sought among the powers may well be that of "a balance of forces in flux"; thus the balance of power is the prevailing current which we must ride; but this does not mean that we cannot navigate a course that will avoid the reefs that spell environmental disaster.

Would that the course we could set would be a simple one—that azimuth drawn between a Scylla and Charybdis that would lead us to a safe harbor. The chart, unfortunately, is not a detailed one: the navigator must, to a large extent, make his own discoveries, and like Dante's Ulysses, be willing, even to the point of danger, to venture beyond the pillars of Hercules to the unknown oceans beyond the safe confines of a known world.

The likelihood, then, is for a world wholly new to the postwar imagination. It is no longer bipolar; even the term "asymmetrical multipolarity"—with its emphasis on the Big Two and its social, economic, and military gradations among Europe, Japan, and China—is inaccurate, as well as cumbersome, to describe what lies ahead. A pattern of many overlapping coalitions seems the most likely contour of our global typography. These coalitions will involve, in some cases, power relationships, such as the central strategic balance between America and Russia; the North–South axis, such as the European–African connection; and finally the movement of transnational forces that will crosscut the traditional modes of balance-of-power considerations. At the same time, the continued viability of the nation-state acts to prevent transnational forces from superseding the ordinary functions of the statist approach. As Stanley Hoffmann has warned:

It is not the use of force which is the daily peril, it is, literally, chaos. It is not war that brings the moment of truth, it is economic or monetary or environmental disaster. It is not failure of the balance to work and curtail excessive ambitions, or the rigidity of the balance when it splits the world into rival, frozen coalitions; it is anomie.[11]

The struggle that results might well be characterized as an endgame in which the players at both chessboards—one statist, the other federalist—can neither resolve the game at hand. Nor is the option of resigning available. Instead, what we have is a situation in which nations lose control over transnational forces—people, money, material, ideas—while other organizations—multinational corporations, foundations, professional and trade organizations—increase their opportunities to utilize resources across national boundaries.[12]

These are irreducible facts that loom before us: private actors, such as multinational corporations, of which more than eighty-five have assets greater than fifty members of the United Nations, often conflict with the interests of the nation-state. Moreover, the amounts of resources that move across international lines, as Louis Wells has pointed out, can fulfill objectives "that may well be at variance with those of a particular country in which a subsidiary is located. These firms have at their disposal many tools for frustrating governmental policies, but the policies they frustrate may be those of the host government or those of the home government." Thus, transnational relations can easily take the form of a postcolonial private economic imperialism.

It is sometimes fashionable to assume that the world would be a better place once the nation-state disappears. But, as Seyom Brown says: "Before anyone gets too enthusiastic about the erosion of national sovereignty heralded by the growth of transnational relations, one should ponder the effect of these trends on the traditional framework for ensuring democratic accountability." The emergence of technocratic authoritarianism is just as dangerous as power relations between and among the nation-states. Certainly the pull to global cartelization does not lead to a world in which we wisely allocate the globe's resources. There is, as Brown stresses, "rather than a just world order gradually evolving out of expanding socio-economic intercourse, the prospect . . . of increasing socio-economic conflict on a worldwide basis."

Where do we stand then? It is clear that we must perceive the world without any illusion that the new transnational forces are creating a form of interdependence among the nation-states that will lead us along the paths of peace and justice.

There are still those reefs that loom ahead of us. They must be navigated, even if they are in the form of a cartel-dominated world, rapacious in its consumption of nonrenewable resources and seemingly beyond our capacity to organize and control; as Margaret Mead stated at the 1972 Stockholm Conference: "so rapid our growth in numbers, so heavy the load we place on our life-supporting systems that we begin to perceive the finite qualities of the biosphere of soil, air, and water . . . this is a revolution in thought fully comparable to the Copernican revolution."

What this leaves us with is a world wherein America, in her search for new directions in her foreign policy, must pursue two lines simultaneously. She cannot disregard the realities of the nation-state and the balance-of-power politics that this implies. At the same time, she must avoid the excesses of neo-nationalism—with its concomitant unilateralism—while finding ways of devising new relationships that will cut across existing alliances.

There is no need to abandon either the European or the Japanese alliance as America searches for ways of cooperation with former ideological antagonists. Although these alliances may become obsolete with the passage of time, such is neither desirable nor likely in the foreseeable future. For one thing a Russo–American or Chinese–American condominium is also neither likely nor desirable. No one would gain from such an arrangement, and the security that the United States provides to both Europe and Japan, while both these latter powers seek to define a more independent role for themselves, can only be reinforced by Washington's willingness to avoid any devolution of an alliance into a client-state relationship. The end of alliance, when it comes, would be the better alternative.

At the same time the United States can and *should* seek new arrangements for cooperation with its ideological adversaries.[13] To do so would involve, as Seyom Brown has said, "resisting temptation to mobilize cold war allies to speak in concert on new issues or have alliance structures form the scaffolding of new institutions." To do so would also mean surrendering a concept of sovereignty which Washington has always been most reluctant to do. Transfers of aid to the poorer countries, the allocation of United States resources to form genuine modes of cooperation with other advanced industrial nations in constructing "global networks for monitoring and regulating the use of the

globe's atmosphere, water, and terrestrial resources to assure that essential ecosystems are not dangerously destabi-
lized"—this will not only require the United States to share
its technological innovations with others but also to involve
the poorer nations at the decision-making level.

SIX

Finally, then, the emerging structure of a new American
foreign policy can be envisaged. America, despite the de-
mise of her imperium, will probably not conclude, as David
Hume said of the Athenians, that "finding their error in
thrusting themselves into every quarrel, abandoned all attention to foreign affairs." On the contrary, what is more
likely is a new internationalism that will probably result in
a series of new involvements rather than a withdrawal into
isolationism.

Thus, the balance of power, despite its dangers and asym-
metry, paradoxically remains the precondition for an
American policy that would transcend the bounds of neo-
nationalism. The Chinese–Russian tensions are not likely to
diminish; the European and Japanese thrust toward independence is likely to continue. Such developments offer opportunities for the United States to work toward some form
of equilibrium that will also allow us to go beyond containment to seek access and influence, not military hegemony,
throughout the world. Such a policy would *not* be aimed at
excluding the other major power centers. It would be a policy that accepts the concept of the nation-state as the most
viable actor on the world's stage. It is also a policy that

makes use of the nation-state to control transnational forces. Despite the urgings of the Secretary General of the United Nations, there is, in fact, no other instrumentality to take its place.

Even when obvious dangers to the environment threaten those shores and waters beyond the confines of the nation-state, the political difficulties of effecting arrangements that would supersede the authority of the great powers have in no way diminished. The most recent example of this was the 1972 Stockholm Conference on the Environment. The Soviet Union refused to attend because the East Germans were not represented. East Germany—the seventh industrial power in the world—was excluded because of the negotiations still in progress to regularize a new political relationship between the two Germanys. It would seem an absurd situation to hold such a conference without the attendance of two such great industrial powers. The key to the control, then, of transnational forces is still held by the nation-state. And the political implications of any balance-of-power system is that without the participation of the great powers, transnational forces are likely to run wild. The very existence of these new forces, however, proves that a static balance would be impossible to achieve. The withdrawal of rich nations into a ghetto would be a dangerous and selfish game; the rapprochement between former adversaries must be sought. But the final arrangements remain political.

Nor need such a dual policy be without domestic support. The concept of balance-of-power politics need not be discredited if the ideological components are removed. Such a foreign policy, freed from ideological crusading or pacifist idealism or military domination, is not without appeal to a

firm domestic constituency. If world politics rested on balance-of-power considerations alone, then indeed the American drive toward a less parochial theme might be thwarted.

But if the politics of the balance of power were not used
to preserve the status quo, but as a precondition for action
that would involve harnessing forces that we have begun to
recognize as destructive and suicidal not only to the continued viability of the nation-state but to any international
schema of world order, then a domestic consensus, shattered
by the Indochina War, might be reconstructed.

Stanley Hoffmann has posed the question of domestic
support solely for a balance-of-power foreign policy starkly:
"Can we," he asks, "develop something we've never been
good at: a diplomacy that is not merely skillful policy but
clever politics? Can we develop around the balance of
power and America's international interest as a player of
that game, the deep support that previously existed first for
isolationism and later for globalism?" [14]

There is good reason for skepticism under these condi-
tions. The lack of consensus among the great powers is itself
a reason to doubt the validity of such a concept as providing
a popularly supported foreign policy. The nationalistic
mode that has been practiced recently reflects a desire for
an equilibrium only to preserve the selfish interests of the
great powers. Moreover, any search merely to establish
order, i.e., the status quo, can indeed imperil a world beset
by revolutionary changes no less dynamic than those un-
leashed by the events of 1848. To build a consensus for a
foreign policy under those premises would probably prove
chimerical. Consensus—even for the two-tiered system that
has been suggested which rejects the status quo—may be

hard to effect. But the passing of the old order necessarily implies debate over what is to emerge.

We return, then, to the image of the navigator. While he cannot always plot an exact course, he must be aware of deviation, variation, and drift as he sets his compass for the safe harbor, or plots his way through the buoys and seamarks of an arduous voyage. Rarely does he hit upon the marker he has previously plotted; but if he is skilled, he will not be too far off his chosen course.

We cannot know the exact contours of the "shelfy Coast" that threatens us: we know only that it involves forces that menace us all. We also know that the prevailing tides and currents are based on the traditional considerations of power, that the ship still flies the flag of the nation-state. These are the irreducible facts. To pretend that the reef is not there is to risk what cannot be risked; to try to steer against the prevailing currents and tides is foolishness. We can only hope that unlike Palinurus, who "scarcely through the gloom the sullen Shadow knew," we can be like the hero Aeneas who, after his pilot has been washed overboard, "takes himself the Helm, and steers aloof, and shuns the Shelf."

This is the choice before us, and this is the world we must confront.

NOTES

1. See James Chace, "Games People Play," *Interplay*, February 1971.

2. Arthur Krock, *Foreign Policy*, No. 7, 1972, p. 48.

3. Charles Gati, "What Containment Meant," *Foreign Policy*, No. 7, 1972, p. 23.

4. See discussion of Palinurus in Cyril Connolly, *The Unquiet Grave.* New York: The Viking Press, 1945.

5. Harry McPherson, *A Political Education.* Boston: Atlantic-Little, Brown, 1972.

6. Alastair Buchan, "A World Restored?" *Foreign Affairs*, July 1972, p. 657.

7. From a forthcoming essay, "Should We Disengage from the Third World?" by Richard N. Cooper and Joseph S. Nye.

8. See Miriam Camps, *International Affairs*, October 1972.

9. Andrew Pierre, "Nuclear Diplomacy: Britain, France and America," *Foreign Affairs*, January 1971, p. 300.

10. *The New York Times*, July 18, 1972.

11. Stanley Hoffmann, "Weighing the Balance of Power," *Foreign Affairs*, July 1972, p. 633.

12. See Seyom Brown, "A Study of Conglomerate Powers that Transcend Nations," *Saturday Review*, May 20, 1972, pp. 64–67.

13. See Seyom Brown, "The Changing Essence of Power," *Foreign Affairs*, January 1973.

14. Stanley Hoffmann, "Will the Balance Balance at Home?" *Foreign Policy*, No. 7, 1972, p. 70.